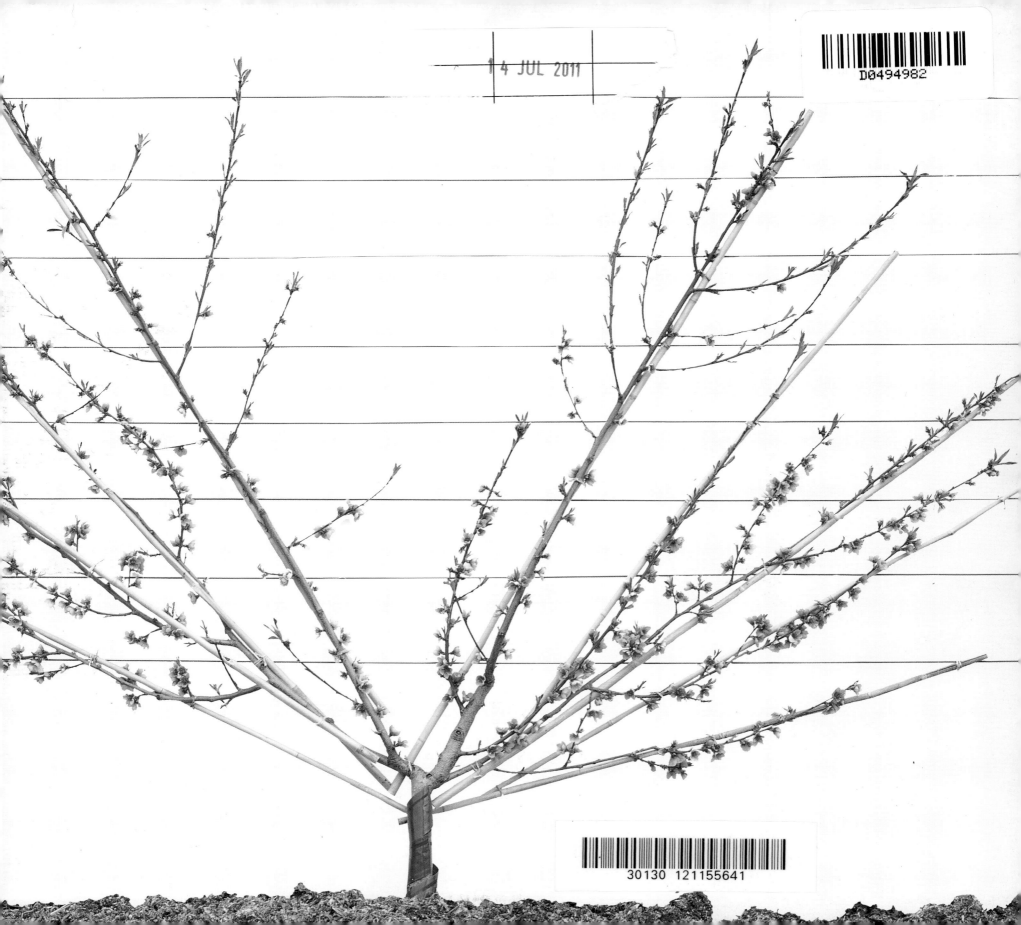

A CREATIVE STEP-BY-STEP GUIDE TO

PRUNING
AND TRAINING

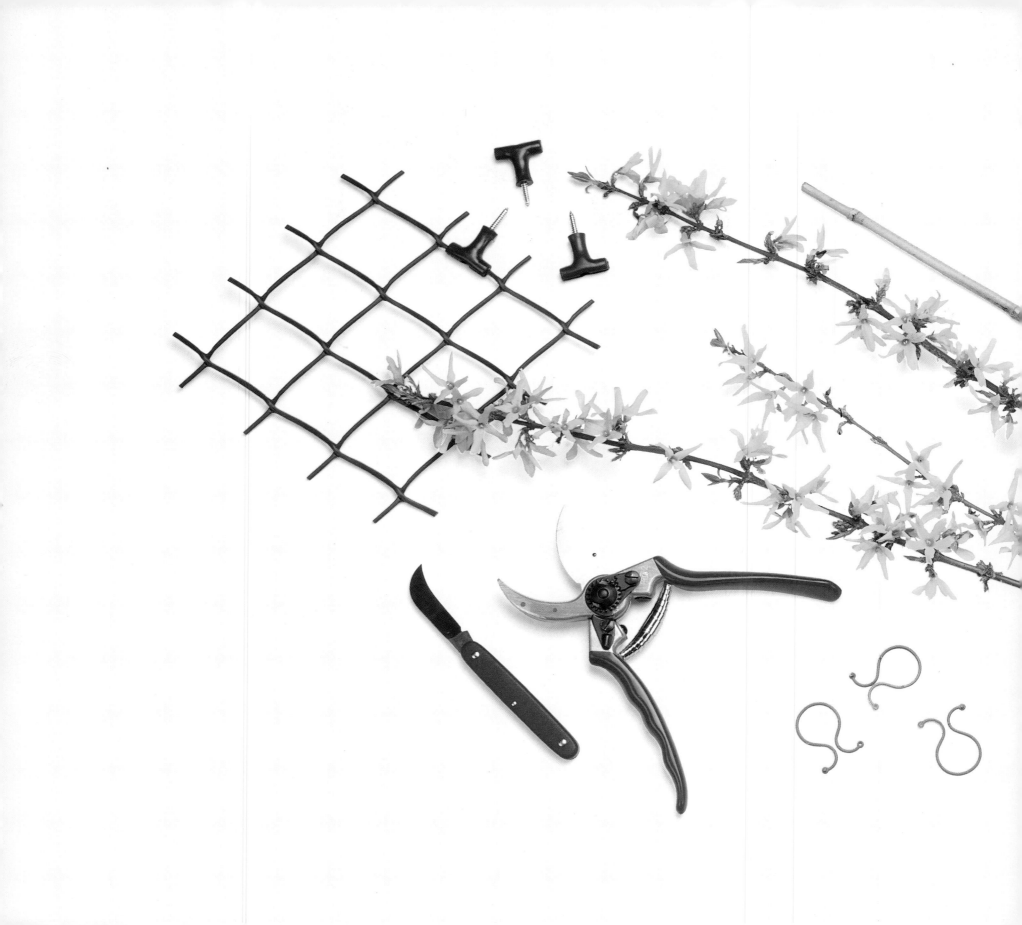

A CREATIVE STEP-BY-STEP GUIDE TO

PRUNING
AND TRAINING

Author
Peter Blackburne-Maze

Photographer
Neil Sutherland

Colour
Library

4535
Published in 1997 by Colour Library Direct
© 1997 CLB International, Godalming, Surrey
Printed and bound in Singapore
ISBN 1-85833-594-1

Credits

Edited, designed and typeset by Ideas into Print
Photographs: Neil Sutherland
Illustrations: Mainline Design and Stuart Watkinson
Production Director: Gerald Hughes
Production: Ruth Arthur, Neil Randles, Paul Randles,
Janine Seddon, Karen Staff

THE AUTHOR

Peter Blackburne-Maze has spent his whole working life in horticulture. He started with growing fruit commercially, but soon widened his experience to take in most aspects of horticulture. Following 11 years in the agrochemical industry, he has, for the past 18 years, been a horticultural consultant and writer. His years in fruit growing gave him a love and fascination for pruning and training trees and he has written several books on the subject. He is a regular contributor to a number of gardening magazines covering ornamentals, fruit and vegetables. He is the current Chairman of the RHS Fruit Group and a member of the RHS Fruit and Vegetable Committee.

THE PHOTOGRAPHER

Neil Sutherland has more than 25 years experience in a wide range of photographic fields, including still-life, portraiture, reportage, natural history, cookery, landscape and travel. His work has been published in countless books and magazines throughout the world.

Half-title page: A fine crop of tasty redcurrants - a feast for the eye in the garden and a treat on the table.
Title page: Early-flowering forsythia provides a vivid spring display; prune after the blooms have faded.
Copyright page: Rosa 'Constance Spry' can be grown as a climber or a shrub, bearing fragrant flowers in midsummer.

CONTENTS

WHY PRUNE?

In any introduction to a book about pruning, there must be an answer to the obvious question 'Why prune at all?' In explaining that, you must understand right away that pruning is not always needed; it doesn't have to be done. If you don't prune a tree or shrub, it will grow adequately but it will not give of its best. You should only prune a tree, shrub, fruit plant, etc., if pruning will improve its performance. Make no mistake, though, correct pruning will certainly improve the performance of any tree or bush. No matter what the plant is, it will grow and operate better.

Pruning has several purposes. To begin with, it induces a plant to grow in the way and into the shape that you want. With a little experience, you soon learn which way a plant should grow to perform best. You could say that pruning is designed to encourage one aspect of a plant's activity. A tree that is planted to beautify a street or garden has to be encouraged to grow. A fruit tree, in whatever shape you want it, has to be encouraged to develop in that shape and then carry crops of fruit. These two operations are achieved by pruning in two different ways. Then again, if you are growing a plant for the shape or color of its young shoots, you prune it in yet another way. All these tactics are described in this book.

To prune correctly and effectively, you need the right tools and you must know how to use them safely and keep them in good condition. Above all pruning is an art that has to be learnt and perfected. You can learn what cuts to make and why to make them but doing this as second nature will only come with time and experience. Above all, never prune simply for the sake of it. Know why you are doing it and do it for a reason.

Left: For a superb display of cornus stems, prune them in early spring. Above: Use sharp secateurs for best results.

Secateurs and other pruners

Above: Loppers are ideal for pruning thick stems where access is difficult, such as at the base of this Berberis thunbergii atropurpurea.

Secateurs are the basic and principal pruning tool. They are used for cutting shoots and small branches up to about 1in(2.5cm) across. The two main kinds are the anvil and the bypass; the names simply refer to the way in which they cut. With anvil secateurs, a single cutting blade presses against a plastic or alloy pad, or anvil. With bypass secateurs, a single cutting blade passes down the side of another blade in a scissor action. The non-cutting blade has a machined edge against which the cutting blade presses, producing a cleaner and more accurate cut with less bruising of the bark. A third kind of secateur, though of the anvil type, is the ratchet kind. These are very useful for gardeners who do not have a very strong grip. They are very easy to use and make short work of cutting through small branches. As with all tools, there are good and bad secateurs and the quality you get depends on the price you pay; anvil pruners are usually cheaper than bypass ones. Loppers and long-arm pruners are all useful but not always essential. Loppers are really secateurs with long handles to give more leverage. Their real use is for cutting shoots and branches that are too thick for secateurs, but where a saw cannot be used easily. Long-arm pruners are invaluable for pruning tall trees or anything that you cannot reach from the ground. In fact, they are almost essential for that purpose, as the only other way to prune the tops is by using a ladder.

These loppers operate on the bypass system; you can buy anvil ones as well. The routine for setting the two blades correctly is the same as that for secateurs of the same design. Because they cut through branches up to 1.5 in(4-5cm) in diameter, it is vital to keep the cutting blade really sharp to avoid injuring the plant.

The anvil principle on which these secateurs work is quite adequate for most pruning jobs but you must keep the blade sharp to avoid damaging plants. Keep the nut in the middle of the secateurs tight, but not so tight that it stops them from working freely.

This ratchet mechanism between the two handles makes these anvil secateurs suitable for any gardener with a weak grip, allowing small branches to be cut with ease.

In bypass secateurs, the sharp cutting blade passes down the side of the non-cutting blade in a scissor action. The two blades must be in contact with each other throughout their length; any gap between them makes cutting more difficult and will leave a tail of bark on every cut you make.

An interesting feature of the ratchet anvil model is that the cutting action of the blade against the anvil is slicing rather than direct force pushing it through. It makes it easier to cut and there is less bruising of the bark.

This is the mechanism that tightens the central bolt. To adjust it, slacken the screw on the locking device and tighten the large central nut (with your fingers if possible) until it will go no more. Test the tightness of the bolt by seeing if there is any sideways play between the two handles. Tighten it further if there is. Make sure that the secateurs open and close fully and, if all systems are 'go', tighten the locking device.

Long-arm pruners

There are two main designs of long-arm pruners: the metal rod type shown here provides a more accurate and precise cutting action than those with a strong cord linking the handle and blade. The pruner will cut through any branches that will fit into the jaw.

Right: Here, the pruner is hooked around the branch that is to be cut off and the cutting blade is halfway through the branch. There is one simple rule about this; if the hooked guide will not fit over the branch, then the branch is too big for the pruner to cut.

Above: With the handle pushed forward, the blade is open and ready to use. It may not be easy to hook a branch at an awkward angle or if there are other branches in the way.

Above: Pulling the handle back closes the blade. If the branch is still attached after pulling the handle fully back, reposition the guide over the branch so that it fits more closely.

Using secateurs

Whatever their quality, the way in which you should use any secateurs is roughly the same; it is just the ease of use and the end result that shows the difference between the models. To get the best from secateurs, there are certain ground rules. The first concerns the size of the shoot or branch that you intend to cut. Although it is annoying to be at the top of a ladder with just secateurs when you find that you could do with a saw, or at least some loppers, do not be tempted to try to cut too large a branch with the secateurs. There can be any of several outcomes. For a start, it will require a great deal of strength, which is not easy up a ladder. Next, you are bound to start twisting the secateurs from side to side, which will damage the wood as well as the secateurs. As if all that were not enough, you could easily lose your temper and fall off the ladder with all the exertion. To use bypass secateurs to best effect, ensure that the anvil is on the outside of the cut and the cutting blade is on the tree or plant side, so that any bruising occurs on the section being removed. Anvil secateurs do an excellent job, but if the blade becomes blunt, you will need more force to drive it through the wood. This causes the anvil to put greater pressure on the branch or shoot and leads to the bark on the underside being crushed. The more damage there is around the cut, the longer it will take to heal.

Loppers are too often wrongly used instead of a saw. They are ideal for removing a complete branch at ground level from bushy plants such as forsythia and blackcurrants. The trouble with this is that, if they are not used properly, they can inflict quite serious damage by leaving crushed and chewed up bark on the bush.

Types of secateurs

Choose the type of secateurs that suit you best. For some jobs, you will need to wear gloves, especially with prickly plants (below).

BYPASS SECATEURS
Below: This shows how bypass secateurs work. When using them, make sure that the cutting blade is on the side facing the plant or tree (here, on the righthand side of the photograph). This means that any bruising of the stem or bark will be on the piece you are cutting off.

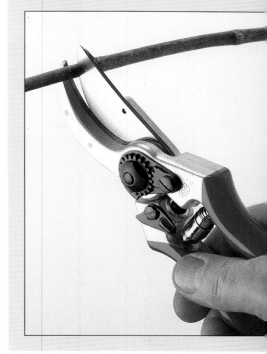

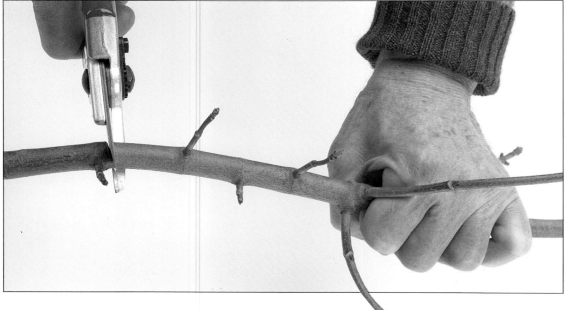

Left: When using secateurs, do all you can to help them cut. Bear down on the branch to keep the cut open so that the blade is not pinched and to help it cut through the wood. Pushing down lightly on the branch puts the wood fibers under tension so that they part more easily.

ANVIL SECATEURS

Right: *The pad (here, plastic) against which the blade cuts is wide so that any bruising will be on both sides of the cut. Hold the blade at right angles to the shoot. The blade is coated for protection and to ease cutting.*

Below: *If you hold anvil secateurs crookedly and apply pressure, the pad will slide along the shoot until it is under the blade. This can crush the bark quite severely.*

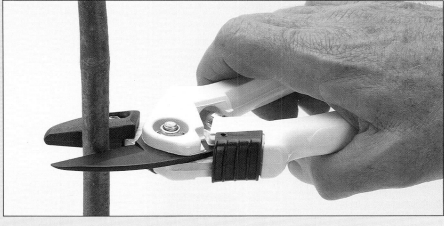

RATCHET SECATEURS

1 *Push the secateurs onto the branch as far as you can and squeeze the handles until they stop. The blade will have started cutting. The click you hear as you release the handles is the ratchet moving up a notch.*

2 *Squeezing the handles again moves the blade further into the branch. Each time you squeeze and release the handles, the secateurs click and the blade slides effortlessly through the branch.*

Left: *Never, under any circumstances, twist secateurs from side to side in an effort to make them cut. All it will do is damage them and cause appalling injury to the wood. Brute force and ignorance is simply not the answer.*

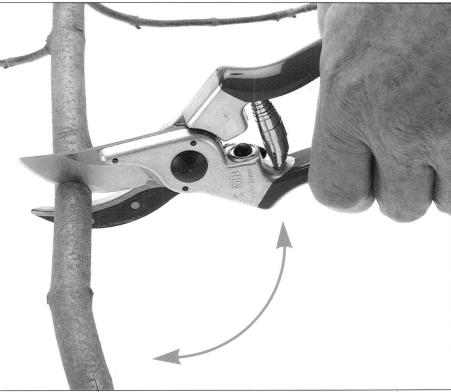

If these techniques are not successful, either the secateurs are blunt or the branch is too thick.

Above: *If the secateurs are having difficulty in cutting, bear down on the branch and, at the same time, move the handles up and down in the same plane as the blade. This will help the blade slice into the wood.*

15

Choosing a good saw

The main thing to remember is that a pruning saw is for pruning and a carpentry saw is for carpentry. Neither saw is suitable for the other use. A good pruning saw will always have the teeth set so that it cuts best when *pulled* towards you, while the teeth of a carpentry saw are set so that it cuts with a *pushing* action. This arrangement exists simply because it is easier, safer and gives the best results. The safety factor comes in when you are pruning up a ladder. A pulling action draws you towards the ladder, a pushing action pushes you away. Unless you are using a modern pruning saw where the teeth are not offset, the teeth are normally larger and give a coarser cut than those on a carpentry saw. The narrower tip of a pruning saw allows you to cut in tighter corners than the deeper blade of a carpentry saw. The only slight exception to this is that, when cutting off large branches, you can use a bow saw if it is convenient in other respects. Having established that a pruning saw should be used only for pruning, the other thing to remember is that, as with knives and secateurs, you must keep it sharp. The edge will stay sharper for longer if the saw is only used for pruning.

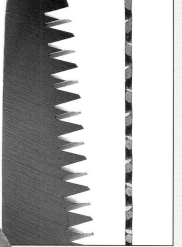

Pruning saws with a curved blade are marginally better because the tip of the blade cuts as effectively as the rest.

Right: *This saw has two cutting edges, one coarse and one finer. The problem with it is that the teeth are usually too large, giving a coarse finish, and, you can cause unintentional damage when the back cutting edge comes into contact with the tree if you prune in a tight space.*

Saw cutting edges

Left: *Offset teeth are designed to prevent the saw binding when you are over halfway through the branch, but they produce an undesirably coarse cut, leading to a very rough finish.*

Right: *The best saws have straight. razor sharp teeth, as it is the edge of the tooth that cuts the wood, not the point. The cutting edge is thicker than the back edge to prevent the saw binding.*

Right: *A very coarse cut will provide a perfect surface for fungal spores to shelter. They can infect the wound, often leading to rot.*

Left: *This remarkably smooth cut end will quickly start to heal over and will not have to be pared down smooth and level with a knife.*

Knives

Knives must always be sharp enough to cut through thin shoots or to pare saw cuts smoothly and evenly. A really sharp knife (or saw) is far less dangerous to use than a blunt one, as it will cut with a lot less effort; it is the rough handling needed to make a blunt tool cut that causes so many accidents.

You might think that one knife is much the same as another, but it is the shape of the blade that is important. This curved one is the most suitable shape for pruning. As you pull the knife towards you to cut through a shoot, the shoot will inevitably be pushed away from the cutting edge. The curved tip stops this happening.

This is an example of a pruning saw with a blade long enough to cut comfortably through branches with a diameter up to about half its length.

A straight blade is fine for cutting everything from string to bits of wood. Additionally, if you should want to try your hand at grafting, the straightness is essential to achieve a flat surface on both parts of the graft.

This model has the hollow ground blade shown on the opposite page. It also has a sheath into which you slide the saw when it is not in use.

Folding saws have several distinct advantages. They are much safer when not in use because the blade folds back into the handle. At the same time, this protects the cutting edge of the blade from accidental damage. They also take up less room. It is normally only the smaller sizes of pruning saw that fold; larger ones may have a sheath instead.

Unless you have the ability and the correct tools for sharpening a saw, have it sharpened properly. If the blade needs to be replaced, look on the pack to see if the manufacturer has a spares service.

Using a pruning saw

Saws should be used for pruning a lot more than they are, as the right saw makes a much neater and better job of cutting through branches than anything else. All too often, loppers or, even worse, secateurs are used to cut through branches that are far too large for anything but a saw. At best, inappropriate tools will damage the tree or bush; at worst, perfectly good tools, as well as the tree, will be ruined. As a guide, it is best to use a saw on any branch more than about 1.25in(3cm) in diameter. You can cut straight through branches of this size at the appropriate place, taking the weight of the branch in your free hand just before it goes. Cut from the top of the branch downwards, using the weight of the branch to keep the cut open, but still controlling the branch with your free hand. If the branch is too big for this, then either make an upward cut first or remove the branch a piece at a time. This last point is very important. You can do a lot of damage if, after cutting through a large branch, you then drag it out in one piece. You will break off shoots, twigs and fruit buds and make a terrible mess of the tree, so saw all large branches into smaller pieces and remove each piece separately. The correct place to make a cut is obviously at the base of the branch being removed, but not flush with it. At the base of every branch you will see wrinkles. Make the cut so that these are left. The bark there grows comparatively fast and the cut will heal over quicker. As with all pruning tools, saws must be really sharp. A blunt saw takes a lot of effort to make it cut and this is when accidents happen. Saw with an easy action and without undue force; you are not in a race.

1 When removing a branch that is too big for you to control fully with your free hand, start by making an upward cut from below at the point where the branch is to be severed.

Removing a branch in two pieces

1 If it is difficult or impossible to make an upward cut before removing a medium-sized branch, cut away the greater part of the branch first. This need not be done carefully.

2 With most of the branch gone, along with its weight, you can now easily cut away the remainder without the risk of tearing the bark. This is also a safer way of working.

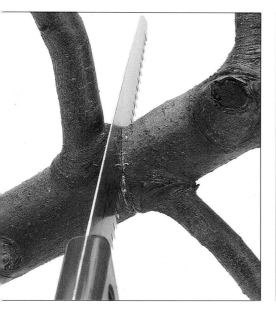

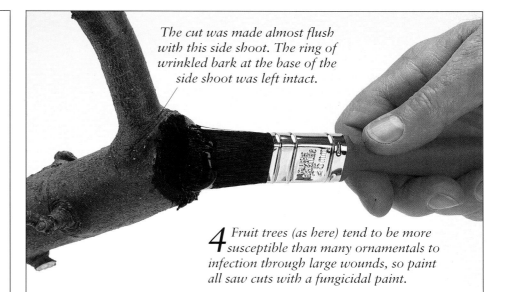

The cut was made almost flush with this side shoot. The ring of wrinkled bark at the base of the side shoot was left intact.

4 Fruit trees (as here) tend to be more susceptible than many ornamentals to infection through large wounds, so paint all saw cuts with a fungicidal paint.

2 Make a second cut above the first so that, as near as possible, they are opposite each other. Just before the two cuts meet, the branch is apt to fall suddenly, so be ready for it.

3 By first cutting the branch from below, you stop it tearing away that tongue of wood and bark that almost always occurs when a heavy branch is cut straight from above.

Paring a saw cut smooth before painting it

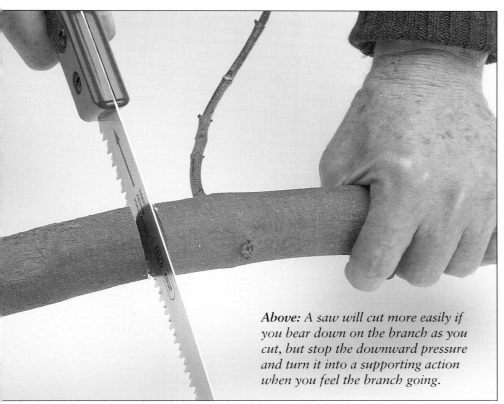

Above: A saw will cut more easily if you bear down on the branch as you cut, but stop the downward pressure and turn it into a supporting action when you feel the branch going.

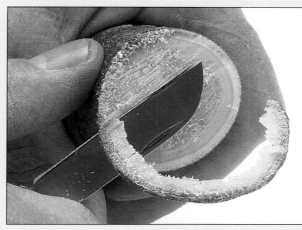

1 If you use a pruning saw with offset teeth, it leaves a rough finish. Pare away the outer edge, where the bark is, with a sharp knife.

2 You can now paint the whole wound and the smoothed edge will start the healing process quicker. There is no need to pare the woody center of the cut before painting.

The principles of pruning ornamentals

Before you prune almost any plant, there are two fundamental questions to ask yourself: 'How will a plant react if I do such-and-such to it?' and 'What should I do to make it do so-and-so?' In most cases, cutting away part of a tree, be it a young shoot or a mature branch, stimulates the plant to grow in the area of the removal and replace the part removed. For example, if a branch breaks or is cut off, a forest of shoots takes its place. This is fine if you want them, as you would with, say, buddleia, but what if you do not? In this case, you must decide whether it is a good idea to remove the branch at all. Shortening it may be more prudent. In other words, every cut that you make must have a purpose. Aimless snipping for the sake of it usually does more harm than good. On the other hand, if you do not cut out a certain branch, then a tree or shrub may become congested and flowering can be reduced because of a lack of young wood. Most flowering woody plants perform best when there is a good supply of new shoots, so removing old branch systems is often beneficial.

The answer to the question of how to make a tree or shrub do what you want is not always so simple, because Nature has a nasty habit of not always complying. A typical example is the shoot that you encourage to grow in a certain direction. You cut it back to a bud that is pointing in the direction you want it to take, but often that bud stubbornly refuses to grow, while the one below takes off like the wind in a completely different direction! That's life. However, there are ways of encouraging a specific bud to grow out and discouraging others. These techniques apply mainly to training fruit trees, but they are useful to know when forming any young tree.

Once you understand these basic principles and apply them to the plants in your garden, you will be able to prune effectively and with confidence.

Right: When you cut off the tip of a shoot, it immediately causes the new top two or three buds to break into growth and form side shoots. This is because you have removed the dominant effect of the former leading bud.

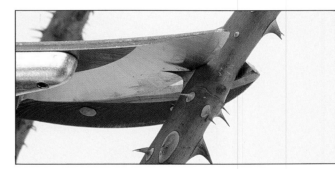

Left: Always prune close to a bud or another shoot so that no snag is left to die back. When using 'scissor' action secateurs, have the blade nearest to the bud and the pad on the outside.

CUTTING TO A BUD

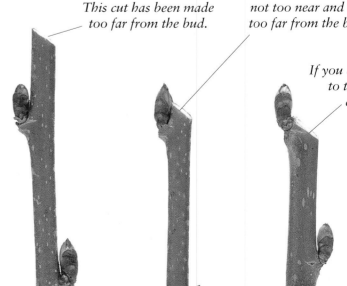

This cut has been made too far from the bud.

This cut is just right; not too near and not too far from the bud.

If you cut too close to the bud, you could kill it.

SHOOTS WITH OPPOSITE BUDS

Right: A shoot with leaves set in pairs behaves in the same way. When its tip is removed, the pair of buds now at the top break into growth. Basically, any shoot reacts like this when its growing point is removed.

These shoots grow out from buds just below where the stem has been cut.

Left: This shoot was cut thoughtlessly, leaving a long snag. It looks untidy and, far worse, it can rot and cause a fungus to spread back into the healthy shoot.

PRUNING TO AFFECT BRANCHING

This branch is growing in the 'desired' direction.

This branch is growing in the 'wrong' direction.

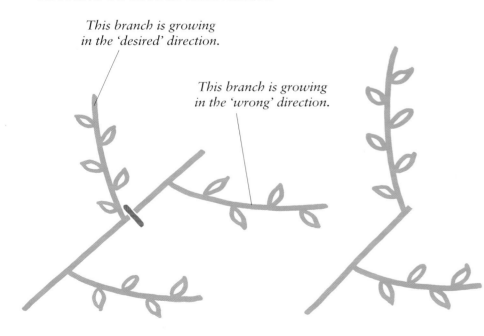

Above: This is a two-year-old shoot bearing side shoots. You can alter its direction of growth to any other

direction by cutting it back to a side shoot that is already growing in the desired direction.

PRUNING TO CHANGE THE SHAPE

Above: Most young woody trees or shrubs can be made bushier by cutting back the central stem to a side shoot.

This makes the new 'leader' (topmost shoot) more upright and encourages it and the lower shoots to grow strongly.

When to prune

Understanding the two principles of pruning explained on page 20 will help you to decide when to prune your trees and shrubs. But another important point to bear in mind is that pruning is not always needed; it isn't compulsory. You should prune a tree, shrub or fruit plant only if pruning will improve its performance and not merely to satisfy a whim. If you do not prune a tree or shrub, no actual harm is going to come to it; it will merely operate less efficiently. This could mean fewer flowers and/or fruit, poorer flowers, less and/or weaker growth, poorer foliage and general untidiness. If you prune something in the wrong way or at the wrong time or, perish the thought, both, then you will do infinitely more damage. On these pages you will find guidance on when to prune ornamental trees and shrubs and fruit.

ROSES
When you prune roses largely depends on when they flower. Tidy bedding varieties (hybrid teas and floribundas) and climbers in the fall and prune them in spring. Prune ramblers soon after their midsummer flowering. Treat shrub roses like other shrubs. Earlies are pruned after flowering and the lates in mid-spring. Prune roses with ornamental hips in spring.

EARLY-FLOWERING SHRUBS
There is no rigid line between early- and late-flowering, but early-flowering shrubs tend to produce their best and/or the most flowers on the previous year's growth. Prune these plants after flowering so that they have the maximum length of time in which to produce new shoots for flowering the following year.

FRUIT
Apples and pears are usually pruned in winter, but trained trees are summer- pruned to encourage the formation of fruiting spurs. Plums and other 'stone' fruit are best pruned after fruit picking to reduce the incidence of 'silver leaf' disease. Most cane fruits are also pruned after fruiting. Bush fruit are usually pruned in early winter but cordons are summer pruned.

HEATHERS
'Clipping' time is governed by when they flower. Prune spring-flowering ericas (heath) in early summer; summer- and fall- flowering ericas in late spring, and winter-flowering ericas and calluna (ling) in mid-spring. They are not really pruned in the classic sense, but clipped with shears or clippers to keep the beds or clumps compact and flowering well.

LATE-FLOWERING SHRUBS

Shrubs flowering after about midsummer flower best on the current season's shoots. Prune them, if necessary, in the spring when growth is starting. This gives them several months in which to produce new shoots to flower later the same year. Do not prune them after flowering, because they would start growing again from the buds at the base of the pruned shoots. These would not mature and harden before the winter months and many would be killed by the cold.

The pruning year

SPRING

Fall raspberries and fruit trees (but not plums) and bushes not pruned in winter. Shrubs that flowered after midsummer, including winter- and early spring-flowering ones. Climbing and bush roses, evergreens and conifers, including cutting back into old wood for rejuvenation. Evergreen and conifer hedges. Shrubs with ornamental stems.

SUMMER

After flowering: almost all spring and early summer-flowering shrubs. Midsummer: cordon bushes of redcurrants and gooseberries. Late summer: cordon, fan and espalier apples and pears. After fruiting: plums and early raspberries. Clip hedges. Deadhead roses (not ones with hips) and other flowered shrubs. Summer prune wisteria. Prune rambler roses.

TREES/SHRUBS WITH FRUITS OR BERRIES

Most are early-flowering to allow time for the berries (botanically fruits) to develop before winter. Pruning after flowering would remove the embryo fruitlets. If needed, prune them in the winter or early spring. The emphasis must be on leaving as much flowering wood as you can; the flowers, after all, develop into the fruits.

FALL

Summer-prune trained fruit trees not mature enough earlier. Later fruiting plums. Hybrid cane fruits and blackberries after fruiting. Summer raspberries not yet done. Cut off dead heads of flowered shrubs. Lightly prune bush and climbing roses and tie in the shoots of the climbers.

CONIFERS

Conifers have their own characteristic shape and any pruning tends to interfere with this and spoil the plant. The main exception to this is conifer hedges. Clip them in spring, but fast-growing ones may need it in summer and early fall as well. If a conifer is damaged, administer first aid immediately (such as tying up) and any serious remedial work in the spring.

ORNAMENTAL SHOOTS

The beauty of these plants, such as Cornus, lies in their juvenile growth, so prune them to produce as many shoots as possible. Mainly, it is the winter shoots that are the attraction, so prune them hard in early or mid-spring. This encourages plenty of new shoots for the following winter.

WINTER

Prune fruit trees (except plums) and bushes after leaf-fall so that you can see what you are doing. Also, trained fruit trees not summer-pruned. Prune most ornamental trees, except winter and spring flowering. Spur back summer-pruned wisteria shoots.

Deadheading

1 *With perpetual flowering roses, deadheading is almost summer pruning. Cut the heads back to either a shoot that has yet to flower or to a bud.*

2 *Having removed half the flowerhead, cut back the other half to a bud. This will usually grow into another flowerhead to carry on the flowering season as long as possible.*

Flowering plants produce flowers as their means of reproducing. The reproductive parts are in the center and the petals are there to attract bees and other pollinating insects. Once the plant is fertilized and the seeds start to form, the petals die and the flower loses its attraction. Because the plant's job is to produce seeds for the next generation, it is reasonable to say that, once seed is formed, no more flowers are needed or produced. On the other hand, if the flowers fail to set seed or if the seedheads are removed, more flowers are produced in a further attempt to form seeds. Now the reason for removing the old flowers soon after they fade becomes clear; deadheading encourages the plant to produce more blooms. In this way, flowers are produced over as long a period as the plant can manage. The main exceptions to deadheading are roses with ornamental hips, plants that produce berries and fruits, and annuals such as teazels, honesty and love-in-a-mist, all of which are partly grown for the seed capsules anyway.

Below: The rules are the same for less showy and smaller types of rose. Here, the fading flowerhead is removed to leave other shoots to produce flowers.

1 Some shrubs have too many flowers to make deadheading feasible. Others do not set seed readily. This escallonia falls into both categories; deadheading is more for looks.

2 Escallonia produces flowers on well-defined heads. Once the flowers are over, remove them to leave just growth shoots.

Above: Camellias have buds behind their single flowers. Avoid damaging them when you remove faded flowers. The buds will grow into shoots and many will flower the following spring.

Below: Rhododendrons also have growth buds behind the flowerheads. Remove old flowers carefully and the buds will grow. If there are too many, thin them to leave what you want.

Below: Spiraea is another borderline case, where deadheading and summer pruning are in conflict. Deadhead small specimens, as here, but prune larger ones in summer.

For small shoots scissors may be easier to use than secateurs.

Dealing with suckers

A sucker is a shoot that usually grows from below ground at the base of a tree or shrub. It nearly always comes from the roots. There are two main kinds, depending on how the 'parent' plant was propagated. If it was budded or grafted, then the sucker will grow from a root system, unlike the main plant. If the parent grew from a cutting, then the sucker will be identical to the parent. With some shrubs growing on their own roots, such as *Chaenomeles,* you could leave the suckers to increase the size of the parent. With budded or grafted plants, such as lilac and many *Prunus,* the suckers will be different to the main plant and must be removed. If left, they will grow very vigorously and could dominate the main tree or shrub. They also take a lot of water and nutrients that should go to the parent plant.

Viburnum

This viburnum, like many others, is growing on a seedling rootstock and the suckers must go. An effort was made to cut off the original one, but it has simply carried on and is growing longer.

This is one branch of the sucker.

These are the shoots of the parent plant Viburnum plicatum 'Mariesii'.

The sucker is Viburnum opulus.

Chaenomeles

Although this plant is growing on its own roots, remove these suckers as they are spoiling the plant's appearance. You could grow them on as rooted cuttings.

This is the parent plant grafted onto the rootstock.

This sucker is growing directly from the root system.

Roses

Most roses are budded onto seedling rootstocks. These two suckers clearly come from the roots. Their leaves are thinner and the shoots are paler. Be sure to remove them.

This thick brown stem is the rootstock with the rose variety grafted to it.

These suckers are clearly growing from the rootstock.

Sucker

Sucker

Above: Suckers must be pulled up so that they bring some of the parent root with them. If they are cut off, the buds left behind will grow out into even more suckers.

Corylus avellana 'Contorta'

This twisted hazel has been grafted onto an ordinary rootstock. It may be enough to cut off the suckers, but it is unlikely to have the desired effect and they will probably grow again - and more strongly. You will then have to dig down around them and pull them off the roots.

Sorbus

These are the suckers from the seedling rootstock of an ornamental Sorbus tree. Although they have been cut off, the cut was made well below ground and they are unlikely to reappear from that point. This is simply because Sorbus, or the mountain ash, rootstock does not sucker prolifically.

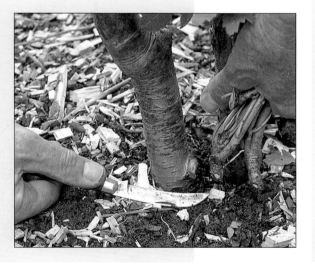

What is training?

Training is not always easy to separate from pruning because, very often, pruning forms a part of training, as in young trees and shrubs. In the main, though, pruning is connected more with the efficient working of a plant, whereas training is definitely a shaping operation. Now shaping may, of course, go hand-in-glove with 'production', as it does with cordon and espalier fruit trees. In this case, the trees not only produce an improved crop when they are trained, they also grow into a pleasing shape. With ornamental trees and shrubs, there are other aspects to consider. For example, some shrubs are best grown against a wall, perhaps to show them off to best advantage, because the appearance of many plants is improved by an attractive background. It could also be to provide the plant with protection from winds and cold, as with *Garrya elliptica*. Then again, you might decide to train a climbing plant as a physical barrier between gardens or sections within a garden. Essentially, training involves making a tree or shrub grow in a way that it would not normally do. This can be done to a degree by pruning away the shoots and branches that are out of place but, sooner or later, you will have to secure shoots and branches in the positions that you want them to be. In its simplest form, this can mean tying one branch loosely to another but, with more formal types of training, you will need to erect some kind of support, such as a trellis or wires, to which you can tie the plant. There are many to choose from and you have to consider carefully the most appropriate kind for your plants. Throughout the book we look at different supports and the various ways of tying shoots and branches to them.

Disbudding

Do not allow side shoots to grow out. Nip out the buds to save the tree wasting energy.

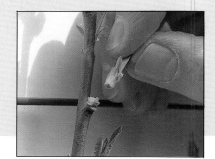

Tying in shoots

Never tie a young shoot to a wire too tightly. The shoot will expand, but not the string. Leave a little slack for this swelling.

Above: *To make a shoot grow in a certain direction, tie string to a fixed point, loop it round the shoot and tie it to another fixed point.*

28

Right: *Step-over apple or pear trees make an unusual sight in an ornamental border. Train them to wires or against a frame of canes. You can use them as garden dividers, too.*

Below: *A fine example of* Buddleia alternifolia *as a flowering standard. To form it, first grow it up a single stem, stopping it and training out side shoots. If necessary, grow it over and round a hoop.*

Pinching out

It is always better to nip out the soft terminal bud on a green shoot rather than wait until it has grown and then have to shorten an overlong shoot.

Above: *You may think it easy to get a climber to grow up a pole, but only a self-clinger will make it unaided. This hop needed string to twine around or it would have ended up on the ground.*

Left: *This beautiful partnership of clematis and* Chaenomeles japonica *(ornamental quince) is made possible by tying the quince to a support and letting the clematis scramble up it.*

Above: *To prune the rambler rose 'American Pillar' growing on an arch, unfasten it after flowering, spread it on the ground, prune off the flowered shoots and tie in the new ones.*

Plant ties

There are a bewildering number of plant ties on the market and various factors will influence your choice. One is price; if you have many plants to train, choose the least expensive tie that will do the job efficiently. String of the appropriate thickness is best. If you only need a few ties, then try one of the more expensive proprietary ties. Consider how long you want the tie to last. If you are tying something that is going to be cut down at the end of the growing season or in the spring, then string may be fine. However, if you are tying the permanent branches of a fan-trained tree or an apple or pear espalier, then one of the stronger plastic ties is going to be better. Take care when using wire ties, even those covered in paper or plastic. Wire has no give in it at all and if allowed to bite into a branch or shoot, the results can be fatal. The same applies to plastic agricultural baling twine. This is especially important when you are securing a free-standing tree to a stake. In this case, use a purpose-made plastic tree tie, which is strong but also has a bit of stretch, so that the tie breaks before it strangles the tree. The strongest kind is like a belt with a buckle on one end. Another sort, though not quite as strong, looks something like a chain. The golden rule with all plant ties is to examine them periodically during the growing season to determine if they are still doing a good job or are beginning to constrict the plant in any way.

Aluminum wire split rings are not very strong but ideal for supple shoots. They expand if the shoots thicken more than you expected in a season.

Inexpensive plastic-covered wire ties are useful for general tying work. Buy them ready cut or on a roll in a dispenser. Check them regularly.

These plastic ties are an adjustable alternative to string for looping young shoots to canes and trellises.

Strong plastic adjustable ties are suitable for tying small branches or the stem of a young tree to a cane or frame.

String is cheap, versatile, can be plain or treated with a preservative, and is available in a range of thicknesses and strengths.

Twist ties

1 *Cut a long piece of plastic-coated wire. To prevent slippage, wind it once around the support before looping it around the plant stem.*

2 *Finish off with two or three twists, leaving the loop slack to avoid constriction. Wire ties are very strong and can soon bite into stems.*

Plastic split rings work on the same principle as aluminum ones and are just as convenient to use.

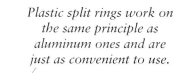

These plastic clip ties are stronger than ring ties. When assembled (see above right) they form a figure-of-eight shape.

These plastic clips are excellent for anchoring stems to overlapping slatted fencing.

Using plastic clip ties

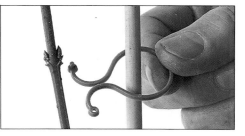

1 *This plastic tie prevents the stem rubbing against its support by having a loop for each. It is very easy to use. Pass the tie around the cane.*

2 *Squeeze the tie to form another loop around the plant stem. Join the two ends by pressing the lug into the hole. It can be used many times.*

Plastic clips for fences

Above: *This clip supports a plant on an overlapping fence panel. Push each end down onto the upper edge of a slat. On the other side of the fence, push the clip up onto the lower edge.*

Using a tree tie

1 *Push the end of the tie through the buckle to hold the tree firmly but not tightly, and away from the stake.*

2 *Push the tie back through the plastic ring to stop it slipping. If plastic ties are stiff, dip them in warm water.*

String ties

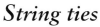

1 *Wind a length of string once round the support and then round the stem. String will only last about a year, so it is less likely to strangle a plant.*

2 *Tie the ends securely with a reef knot. Some thicker grades of string are very soft and there is little risk that they will chafe soft plant stems.*

3 *Snip off the ends of the string fairly close to the knot for tidiness. This brown string has been tarred to make it last longer in all weathers.*

Training accessories

As well as the vast array of plant ties available today, there is also a wide range of accessories designed to enable the whole process of supporting plants to be carried out more effectively and smoothly. These items are not really supports in themselves, nor are most of them ties for joining plants to their supports. But they do make the whole task of attaching plants to different surfaces easier and often their appearance is a great improvement on the older materials that were once commonly used. On these pages we present an overview of some of the products you may come across. Using your own initiative and imagination, you can probably add some solutions of your own. One of the best materials to have been developed over the years is plastic mesh. It is much more attractive and pleasant to handle than the galvanized wire netting it has replaced, and easier for most plants to climb up. Plastic-coated wire is another great improvement on the old galvanized type. Some things, of course, can never be 'plasticized', because only metal has the necessary strength. Foremost among these are the 'vine eyes', so-called because they were originally devised for keeping the training wires away from the glass and walls in vinery glasshouses. Today they are used in any situation, inside or out, where wires are set out from a wall or fence. Drive them into brick walls and pass wire through them to form the basic support for many climbers and wall shrubs. Trained fruit trees and bushes are also trained to wires. The more expensive screw-in vine eyes have no sharp edges that might damage coated wires.

As well as being easy to handle and good looking, extruded plastic mesh is also available in a choice of colors.

This little gadget holds the plastic mesh onto but away from the wall or fence. Screw in the spacer and press the mesh into the groove on top of it to hold it in place. If necessary, you can move the mesh, with the climber still on it, away from the wall or fence.

Wall ties

Above: *This plastic tie secures a shoot to a wall. Hammer the nail through the hole in the tie, pass the tie around the shoot and pull the tie through the slot. Tighten it as necessary.*

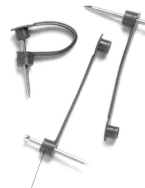

Plastic ties, complete with masonry nails, are suitable for wood, brick or breeze block. Drive the nail in, bend the plastic loop around the plant stem and 'pop' the lug into the nail head.

Three different sizes of 'vine eye' used to hold wire away from a wall. It is easier to tie shoots to the wire if it is not pressed flat against a wall and better for the shoots to be held away from the surface.

These adjustable plastic ties are effective and easy to use.

Galvanized wire is less expensive than plastic-coated, but just as effective.

Medium-strength plastic-coated wire is fine for most purposes.

Right: *White plastic netting blends with the white wall behind it and provides an ideal support for the scrambling plant Plumbago auriculata.*

Although intended as the anchor points at the two ends of a training wire, screw eyes will do the same job as vine eyes, especially on a wooden fence.

Lead-headed nails are used almost exclusively on brick walls. They have a considerable amount of give and move as the shoot expands.

Leaded nails

Training wire is available in several strengths and with different coverings. Thicker gauges are stronger but are more difficult to work with.

Thinner wire may not always be appropriate, though it is certainly the easiest to manage.

Above: *Drive the nail into the wall and place the shoot under the tongue. Bend the tongue to form a hoop with the shoot inside it.*

Fixing wires between posts

Walls and fences are far from the only supports on which to train plants. A row of posts with three or more strands of wire between them can form the perfect boundary between one part of your garden and another or even along the boundary line between you and a neighbor. In this case, roses or blackberries, for example, can be trained to the wire to form an impenetrable barrier after very few years. However, you must set up the whole support system properly so that it lasts a long time and the wires remain taut. First mark out a straight line where the row of posts is to go with strong, tight twine. Push a stick in every 12-15ft (3.7-4.5m) along the wire to mark the position of each post. Secure the posts, ideally with steel fence spikes driven into the ground. These support the post and prevent it rotting. Traditionally, posts were anchored in the ground with concrete, but the posts do tend to rot off in time. Depending on how tall you want the wires to go, 10ft(3m) is a good length for the posts to be so that 2ft(60cm) can be buried, leaving an 8ft(2.4m) post above ground.

1 Nail a small piece of wood across the inner face of the post 2-3ft (60-90cm) from the ground. A supporting strut will eventually push against this block.

3 Now the strut will not move up and down, but to prevent it moving sideways and out of position, drill a hole through the strut and just into the post.

Anchoring the strut

The effectiveness of the strut depends on firm anchorage underground. Estimate the position of the base of the strut before you nail the strut to the post. Dig a sloping hole. After nailing, place a brick under the base of the strut and firm it in as hard as possible. Fill in the hole with earth. Bury the brick a good 6in(15cm) below ground for strength. Repeat the operation with the other end post.

2 Cut the top of the strut at a 45° angle and saw off the sharp edge. Place it under and against the wood block. The strut should be as thick as the post so that it is neat and strong.

4 Put a 4in (10cm) nail into the hole and, making sure that the strut and the post are properly lined up, drive the nail firmly home into the post.

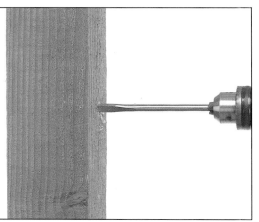

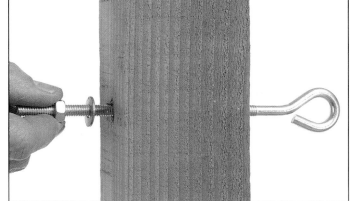

5 *Drill holes at 12in(30cm) intervals for the straining bolts. The lowest wire could be 18in(45cm) from the ground, the highest 6-8in(15-20cm) below the top of the post, depending on what you plan to grow.*

6 *Put a bolt through each hole and begin to screw on the nut. Drill the holes in the other end post at exactly the same distances as in the first post. Make the wires between the posts as near parallel to the ground as you can.*

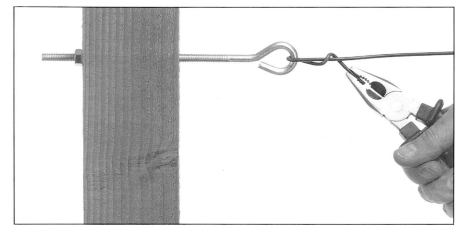

7 *When all the bolts are in place, loop the free end of a roll of wire into the top or bottom bolt. Unroll the wire to the other end post, allowing an extra 8in(20cm) before you cut off the length. Do the same for the remaining wires.*

8 *When all the wires are hand tight on both end posts, start tightening the nuts with a wrench. Begin with the top wire and work your way down. It takes a bit of fiddling to get all the wires to the same tension, but a little practice soon makes perfect.*

9 *The golden rule is to tighten each wire a very little at a time. If you overtighten just one, all the others will need attention. A proper job well done will last for many years.*

Using trellis panels

Trellises are available in an enormous range of shapes and sizes and are some of the most useful devices for supporting climbing plants. Even when empty they are attractive in their own right and when painted or stained they can look even better. However, if this is done badly they can look awful. The natural wood look is probably the best. You can use trellis panels in many ways. They can be erected between posts in the open garden to form a barrier without any plants at all, but it is when they are fixed to a house or garage wall and used to train plants up that they are at their most useful and best. The simplest way of fixing them to a wall is to drill holes through the battens and screw these directly onto the wall. The most important thing is to make sure that they are firmly secured; a collapsing trellis, especially a large one, can be a fearsome thing in a gale.

Hinged panels

Above: Attach battens firmly to the wall to align with the top and bottom of the panel. Fix a hook-and-eye catch at each corner to secure the top edge to the batten.

Above: Fix the bottom edge to the batten with hinges. You can then unhook the top and swing the panel away from the wall for decoration and repairs.

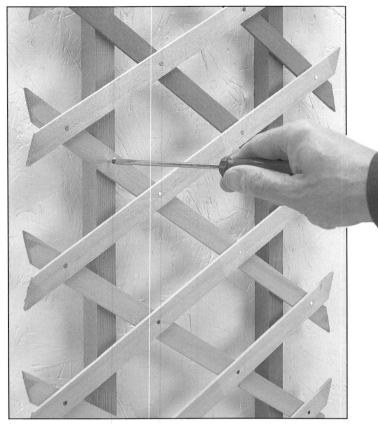

Above: Expandable trellis panels are fairly flimsy and need support if they are to stay put. But they do have the advantage of being adjustable in size to fit most places. Screw them onto fixed battens.

Left: This is a beautiful example of a trellis used as a free-standing plant support. It has been treated with a dark stain and this color contrasts superbly with the gold of the ornamental hop's attractive foliage.

Left: These thicker trellises can be fitted with the vertical or horizontal slats against the wall or fence. However, with the horizontal ones facing the wall, plants may have trouble climbing the vertical battens.

Left: With the vertical battens against the wall, twining plants and climbers can get behind the horizontal slats, as if the trellis were a ladder. Plants tied to horizontal slats are less likely to move.

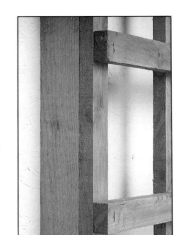

Left: With battens fixed permanently to the wall, you can choose which way to fix the trellis. In both cases, there is plenty of room behind the trellis for plants to climb and to tie up non-climbing shrubs.

Above: Here are two roses growing together and showing how attractive they can be. The two pinks of 'Pink Perpétué' and 'New Dawn', both climbers, are shown off to perfection. Who could resist them?

Right: A very different combination of plants and method of support. Clematis 'Royal Abundance' and Rosa filipes 'Kiftsgate' living in perfect harmony on a wire archway will add height to any garden.

Creating a standard ribes

1 *Find a single-stemmed plant in a nursery or root your own cutting. To form a standard, cut off the tip of the stem at the required height.*

2 *Leave only the top five side shoots. Pinch out the tips when they are 2-3in(5-7.5cm) long, and subsequent side shoots when they reach that size.*

Once the head has developed, only trim to shape after flowering or the following year's flowers will be lost.

3 *Keep well fed and watered, and in a sheltered spot in some sun until the head is well formed. At this stage the tree can be planted out. It is worth tying the stem to a stake for extra support.*

Growing standards

Growing any kind of plant as a standard is no harder or easier than growing a plant in any other shape. An enormous number of different plants can be grown and trained as standards: roses, fuchsias, gooseberries, red- and whitecurrants, wisteria and certain willows and weeping forms of other plants are just a few examples. A standard is just a plant with a longer than usual stem so that, instead of the lowest branches being only just above the ground, the stem is grown straight, without allowing any side shoots to form. When it reaches the desired height, nip out the top and the branches start to grow. There are different optimum heights of stem, but 3ft(90cm) is usual. Another difference is that species vary in the time they take to reach the required height.

For example, quick-growing plants, such as willows, will achieve it in one growing season, whereas, say, a gooseberry will take perhaps three seasons. Fuchsias are very popular as standards. When choosing a cutting to grow into a standard, try to find a shoot with three leaves at a node instead of the usual two. When it starts growing, keep it as a single shoot and tie it to a cane as soon as possible. As it reaches the required height, snip out the tip. Side shoots will start to grow out and away you go.

Right: *Look closely at the top of the stem of a standard rose and you will see that the flowering part has been grafted on. Most gardeners are better off buying ready-made standard roses.*

A standard fuchsia

1 *Gently bring the cutting in close to the stick. Use a soft tie to avoid damaging the tender growth. Keep the stem as straight as possible; it is particularly supple at this stage.*

2 *When the plant has reached the required height, remove the growing tip with scissors. Leave the leaves on the main stem.*

3 *With the top removed, side shoots start growing out. Allow them to produce two or three pairs of leaves, then pinch out their growing tips. This will produce an even bushier top.*

4 *As the bushy head forms, remove the large leaves on the main stem. Gently break off any small side shoots growing on the main stem away from the head.*

Right: *The weight of the large double flowers on 'Royal Velvet' gives the fuchsia a weeping shape. It may need the extra support of a central cane.*

Early-flowering shrubs

For the purpose of pruning, 'early-flowering' shrubs are those that flower before about midsummer. The correct and only way to find out which group a shrub belongs to is to look at the shoots with the best flowers. If these are the shoots that grew in the *previous* year (e.g. *Forsythia*), then the shrub is described as 'early-flowering'. If the best flowers are on shoots that grew earlier in the *same* growing season (e.g *Buddleia*), then it is 'late-flowering'. Shrubs that flower best on the previous year's shoots should be pruned straight after flowering to give the plant the longest possible time in which to produce long, vigorous shoots for flowering in the following year. Thus, a forsythia flowering in mid-spring will have the whole of the growing season until late fall to produce the following year's best flowering shoots. Remember, though, it is only the best flowers that will be produced on the new shoots; there will still be plenty of flowers on older shoots but they will not be of the same high quality. Pruning consists of cutting back or completely removing the oldest branch systems in the shrub each spring after flowering. This opens up the shrub and encourages the formation of new shoots and, at the same time, gets rid of some of the oldest and poorest flowering shoots. Pruning this group in the winter is entirely wrong, as it simply takes away flowering wood; leave it until after flowering.

Above: Winter jasmine (Jasminum nudiflorum) *will only produce such a profusion of high-quality flowers in winter and early spring if you cut the flowering shoots back every year when the flowers have faded.*

WINTER JASMINE

The flowers are only produced on the previous year's shoots. Cut these hard back after flowering. Plants left to their own devices seldom flower well.

1 *Immediately after flowering, cut out all the weak, dead or dying shoots, regardless of whether they have flowered or not.*

2 *Cut back all the strong shoots that have flowered to about 1in(2.5cm) long, just leaving those that you want to keep to increase the size of the plant.*

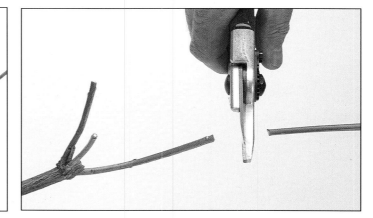

3 *When a shoot of winter jasmine reaches the length that you had planned for it, treat it just like any other shoot that has flowered and cut it back to a pair of strong buds.*

FORSYTHIA

Although pruning is by no means essential, removing the oldest branches to keep forsythia bushes young produces the best results.

Below: There is no room left for more flowers on this Forsythia x intermedia 'Lynwood' bush. It is the result of correct pruning at the right time of year to keep the shrub young and free-flowering.

CAMELLIA

Hardly any pruning is needed and, indeed, camellias object to hard pruning. Restrict it to the removal of out-of-place and over-vigorous shoots.

Below: Pruning this Camellia x williamsii 'Carolyn Williams' for shape has produced a fine show of blooms.

These are the strong new shoots that should be encouraged to grow. Removing old flowering shoots gives them a chance to thrive.

Right: Forsythia makes a good hedge; the snag is that it must be clipped in winter, just before it flowers, to keep it tidy. This form is created by first training suitably placed branches into the desired shape.

41

WEIGELA

Weigela is typical of many early-flowering shrubs in that its best flowers, and the greatest number, are produced on the young wood. Pruning must be aimed at encouraging growth as well as flower production, so prune mature bushes straight after flowering by cutting the oldest branches out or back .

Below: Weigela 'Florida Variegata', a compact, deciduous shrub with decorative leaves and good flowers.

SENECIO

To maintain a supply of the young gray foliage, prune lanky specimens hard in spring when growth starts, even though it reduces the flowers for that year.

Below: Brachyglottis Dunedin Hybrids Group 'Sunshine' (syn. Senecio 'Sunshine') thrives well in a warm, sheltered spot.

POTENTILLA

Summer pruning after the first flush of flowers is usually best. Keep the bushes compact, as they quickly become untidy if neglected.

Below: Potentilla fruticosa 'Tangerine' is typical of many shrubby potentillas that do well in a sunny position.

Left: *If the plant is a good shape to start with, cut out a high proportion of the flowered shoots after flowering.*

Left: *Removing the flowered shoots each year ensures a compact shrub full of young shoots carrying bright foliage and, the following year, abundant flowers.*

PHILADELPHUS

Although it flowers earlier than weigela, prune philadelphus as for weigela. Cut back a proportion of the oldest branch systems every year after flowering to keep the bush young and full of flowers.

Below: Philadelphus 'Beauclerk' is more compact than the more common P. coronarius *but it shares its heady, mock orange scent in early summer and tolerance of dry soils.*

1 Potentilla often looks untidy and in need of attention in the summer, when it is resting after early flowering. This is a good time to prune it.

2 Simply grab a handful of shoots and cut them back as far as you like. However, remember that hard pruning delays the next flowering.

3 An enforced mid-season rest revives many shrubs; it encourages them to flower all the better later on.

Generally speaking, magnolias dislike being pruned. Restrict it to shaping and removing shoots that are actually causing problems.

Below: Because of the brittleness of magnolia wood, some breakages may occur. Repair these and remove any large, broken branches in midsummer to aid healing before the winter.

Above: Cut back up to a third of the older branch systems of Spiraea 'Arguta' in early spring. This leaves the rest of the growing season for the new, long, arching shoots to be produced.

Below: Prune back the flowered shoots, not the branches, of Cytisus scoparius fairly severely to encourage side shoots. Never cut back into older wood; it seldom produces new growth.

Early-flowering shrubs

The shrubs described below are generally pruned in spring, after they have flowered on shoots that grew in the previous year. This has the effect of keeping the plants young, compact and shapely and encourages healthy new growth to form. Only prune a shrub if it actually needs it!

Berberis *Cut out old branches in late winter to keep the bushes open and young. Do this after flowering or in mid-spring for evergreen varieties.*

Buddleia globosa *Remove weak, twiggy growth in early spring to leave mainly strong shoots for flowering. If hard pruning is required, do it after flowering.*

Camellia *No regular pruning needed. Remove or cut back over-vigorous shoots that spoil the shape of the bush as appropriate in mid-spring.*

Ceanothus *Cut back wayward shoots on spring-flowering bushes. On trained plants, cut back all outward-growing shoots shortly after flowering.*

Chaenomeles japonica *Thin out overcrowded branches in bushes. With trained specimens, cut side shoots hard back after flowering. Trim hedges when blooms fade.*

Choisya *If old bushes become leggy, cut them back quite hard after flowering and shorten long side shoots on wall specimens at the same time.*

Cornus *For ornamental winter shoots, prune hard back to 2-3in (5-7.5cm) as growth starts in spring. Shrubby species seldom need pruning.*

Corylopsis *After bushes have flowered, remove the oldest branches, together with weak and twiggy ones. Keep them young and vigorous.*

Cytisus *(some) After flowering, snip back the young shoots that carried the flowers to keep them compact. Never cut into older wood, which seldom sprouts.*

Daphne *No regular pruning is needed or desirable. Simply cut back any long shoots in early spring if they are spoiling the appearance of the bush.*

Erica carnea *Clip the winter-flowering heather with shears after flowering to remove the dead flowerheads, tidy up the plants and keep them compact.*

Forsythia *Cut out one or two old branches from F. x intermedia every year after flowering. With F. suspensa, cut back surplus long shoots at the same time.*

Garrya *Little pruning is needed except to keep the bush shapely. Cut back long and out-of-place shoots on trained specimens in spring after flowering.*

Helianthemum *Cut back or completely remove long, straggly shoots after flowering, along with the dead flowers. Aim to keep plants compact and young.*

Kerria *After flowering, cut back a high proportion of flowered shoots to the ground. Shorten the remaining ones by a third to a half to keep them within bounds.*

Magnolia *Only cut back deciduous species if they really need it and then in summer, as wounds are slow to heal. M. grandiflora tolerates harder pruning if needed.*

Mahonia *Occasionally cut back the tall and showy species after flowering to prevent legginess. Clip low-growing M. aquifolium once a year in mid-spring.*

Malus *Some branches may need to be thinned or shortened when trees are young to create a good shape. Thereafter, the aim is to prevent overcrowding.*

Philadelphus *Each year after flowering, cut back as many of the flowered shoots as possible, together with one or two older branches, to keep the bushes looking young.*

Piptanthus *In late winter, cut out old and worn-out wood and shorten the long young shoots by about half. On trained plants, prune side shoots back hard.*

Potentilla *This shrub starts flowering in early summer on last year's shoots. Cut these back once the flowers have faded to encourage a second flush. See also under late-flowering shrubs.*

Prunus *(ornamental) Beyond shortening vigorous shoots to retain a good shape, little pruning is needed. Do any after flowering to reduce the risk of 'silver leaf' disease.*

Rhododendron *(inc. azaleas) No regular pruning but when leggy, cut back hard in mid-spring. Deadhead after flowering, taking care of the emerging shoots behind the flower head.*

Ribes *Keep the bushes young and compact by cutting out some older branches every year after flowering, together with any that are spreading out or up too far.*

Rosa *Specie and shrub roses flower from mid-spring onwards. Many are grown for their hips as much as for their flowers. Prune them all in early spring.*

Spiraea *Early-flowering varieties, such as S. 'Arguta', are best kept young by removing old branches and cutting back others to younger shoots after flowering.*

Pruning late-flowering shrubs

Late-flowering shrubs produce their best flowers on shoots that have grown during the current growing season. Prune these shrubs, if necessary, in the spring shortly before, or as, growth starts. This gives them several months in which to produce and ripen the new shoots before flowering halts their growth. If you pruned these subjects straight after flowering, almost all the new shoots that grew out after the hard pruning would be killed during the winter. This is worse for the plant than if it had been left alone, because there will be far fewer strong buds left to grow out. You can carry out a secondary pruning (as with bush roses), in early winter to remove dead flower-heads and any breakages. This only applies to plants that look untidy or are liable to wind rock.

BUDDLEIA
First build up a strong, well-spread-out framework of permanent branches to carry the curving flower stems. Next, cut back the flowered shoots very hard every spring to encourage new growth. If neglected, the bush becomes straggly and flowers poorly.

Right: Pruned correctly, Buddleia davidii produces superb tall, arching shoots of scented flowers.

Pruning a young buddleia

1 *Establish a sturdy framework for the new plant by cutting back the main shoots to a suitable length in spring. This will determine the future shape of the bush.*

2 *The newly pruned plant looks rather pathetic now, but by the fall there will be several new, tall, flowering shoots. As it grows, it will achieve the desired shape.*

1 *When flowering is over in the fall, cut back the main shoots to remove the dead flowerheads. Leave the rest of the shoot as winter protection.*

2 *In the spring, cut back all the shoots to no more than 4in(10cm). Cutting back to strong buds is more important than the actual length, but the stubs must be left short.*

LAVATERA

Prune lavatera in much the same way as Buddleia davidii. *Shrubby lavatera is barely hardy in cold climates and needs the protection of its old stems in winter.*

Below: *This shows admirably the amount of growth that lavatera, such as this 'Barnsley', can make in a single growing season. The flowers are produced towards the ends of the tall shoots.*

Above: *It is vital to leave the stems alone after flowering to protect the base of the plant through the winter. Cut away the dead stems when the new shoots start to grow.*

Above: *After pruning, only the new growth remains. Do not be too eager to cut back the dead stems; a cold spring can damage the new growth if it is exposed too early.*

Above: Fuchsia *'Santa Cruz'.* *Pruning encourages new growth and abundant flowers.*

FUCHSIAS

In warmer areas, fuchsias will grow as specimen shrubs and even hedges. Cut the dead growth back to living tissue. If they are killed to the ground in winter, treat them as for lavatera.

Cut back the woody stems as close as you can to avoid leaving dangerously sharp stumps. Do this in spring when the new shoots have started to grow.

Pruning lavender

In midsummer, snip off the dead flowerheads individually and dry them or, as here, trim them with shears. This is quick and leaves shrubs and hedges neat and tidy.

Above: In a dry situation, the scent of lavender is magnified. It needs regular pruning after flowering to stop it becoming sparse and leggy. It is not a particularly long-lived plant, so replace it when it starts to deteriorate.

Right: Escallonia flowers on the previous year's new shoots, but in early and midsummer. Any pruning is for rejuvenation of the bush and for shape. Do it straight after flowering, when you can cut some of the flowered shoots back to a younger shoot further back.

Above: *Witch hazel (Hamamelis) needs little if any pruning, just tidying up. If suckers develop from below ground, dig down and pull these off at once.*

Left: *As growth starts in spring, remove any dead wood and the older, worn out branches of Hypericum 'Hidcote' to keep it looking young and in good shape.*

Late-flowering shrubs

On the whole, late-flowering shrubs flower from midsummer onwards on shoots that have grown during the current growing season. It is fairly safe to assume that all ornamental shrubs in this category not mentioned below are pruned just before or as growth starts in the spring.

Buddleia davidii *In mid-spring, cut the flowered shoots back hard to about 4in(10cm) to encourage strong new ones. Cut flowers as they fade and lightly trim flowered shoots in the fall.*

Ceanothus *Late-flowering ones, such as 'Gloire de Versailles', thrive on hard pruning. In early to mid-spring, remove weak shoots and shorten the remaining side shoots to 6-12in(15-30cm).*

Cistus *Older specimens need little pruning and, indeed, object to it most strongly. It is usually better to replace old bushes, as they seldom rejuvenate.*

Deutzia *In summer, as flowers fade, remove flowered branches with no young side shoots and the occasional old branch.*

Escallonia *No regular pruning, but lightly cut back bushes after flowering or in the spring. Cut back side shoots on trained plants after flowering.*

Fuchsia *If the top growth has been completely killed by the winter, cut all shoots back to ground level as soon as new growth appears in the spring. In mild districts where top growth survives the winter, cut back to strong new shoots in spring.*

Genista *Late-flowering brooms, e.g. G. hispanica, need little pruning. Remove or cut back long shoots in early spring.*

Hamamelis *Only prune when necessary by shortening extra-long new shoots that spoil the shape and symmetry of the bush.*

Hebe *Deadhead after the flowers fade. If hard pruning is required, do this in mid-spring.*

Hibiscus *In spring, shorten the odd young shoot of H. syriacus to encourage branching.*

Hydrangea *Leave the dead flowerheads of the 'hortensia' (mophead) kinds until the spring to protect the flower buds. Cut out weak and twiggy shoots after flowering.*

Hypericum *(shrubby). During early and mid-spring, shorten the previous year's strong shoots by a quarter or more. Otherwise, just aim to keep the bushes tidy and compact.*

Lavandula *Cut off the old flower stalks and trim the bushes in late summer after flowering. If any hard pruning is needed to correct legginess, do it in spring.*

Lonicera *To keep shrubby winter honeysuckle young and relatively compact, shorten over-vigorous flowered shoots in the spring.*

Potentilla *Remove some old branches in fall after flowering.*

Rosa *Bedding and rambler roses are the main late-flowering kinds. Tidy up bedding (H.T. and floribunda) roses in the fall and prune them in spring. Prune ramblers after flowering. For details, see pages 54-59.*

Viburnum *(some). No regular pruning is needed. Remove out-of-place shoots and cut back over-vigorous ones. Do this in mid-spring for fall- and winter-flowering kinds and evergreens.*

Pruning a garden hydrangea

Although most late-flowering (after midsummer) shrubs bloom best on the current season's growth, the well-known, mid- to late summer-flowering *Hydrangea macrophylla* Hortensia and Lacecap varieties produce their best flowers on the strong, young shoots that grew the year before. In fact, they will flower perfectly well if left unpruned but they become large and untidy. Pruning them encourages a plentiful supply of good-quality flowers and keeps the bush looking neat and tidy. Carry out the pruning in spring once the worst of the winter is over and also remove any shoots or tips that have died during the winter. An unusual feature of the Hortensia shrubs is that the old flowerheads are left on until the spring pruning to add winter protection for the terminal buds that produce the summer flowers. The Lacecap varieties are deadheaded once their flowers have faded. If the flowers are left on, they set seed, which will weaken the plant.

Pruning mainly involves removing any large and old branch systems that have grown too tall and are past their best as far as flower production is concerned. Either cut these back to a younger section growing out from near the base or remove them completely.

Prune *Hydrangea petiolaris*, the climbing hydrangea, by shortening back the longer and more obtrusive flowering shoots to a strong bud nearer their base. With a large plant, it is a good idea to stagger the pruning over three to four years as it removes the current season's flower buds.

Below: This is the result of correct and timely pruning - a good show of large flowerheads on a well-shaped, attractive mophead hydrangea.

1 *An unpruned hydrangea soon after growth has started in spring. Last year's dead flowers are still in place, having protected this year's flower buds.*

2 *Cut back the dead flowerheads to a strong growth bud. If necessary, cut back as far as 6in(15cm), or even further, to find a strong bud or to shorten an extra long, untidy shoot.*

3 *When pruning the Hortensia hydrangeas, leave as many of the large terminal buds (those on the ends of shoots) as you can. It is these that will produce the summer flowers.*

4 *With nearly all the old flower-heads gone, think about reducing any congestion inside the bush. Over-crowding leads to weak and spindly shoots that are less likely to flower.*

As in all cases, cut back to a strong bud or leaf.

Hydrangea macrophylla

5 *By now, you will be able to see if there are any outer branches that need to be shortened or completely removed. These are usually the ones that are spoiling the shape of the bush.*

6 *With all the old flowerheads, overcrowded and out-of-place shoots gone, the result is a well-balanced, shapely bush that should flower profusely.*

Foliage trees and shrubs

Whereas flowering trees and shrubs are clearly grown for their flowers, foliage specimens are grown for the beauty of their leaves. A large number of them are trees, such as many of the hollies and sycamores. They have variegated or golden foliage and this obviously adds to their attraction. However, they need little pruning and any that is required is usually the same as for their less attractive cousins with plainer foliage.

Here we are more concerned with the 'trees' and shrubs that are cultivated for their juvenile foliage; their one-year-old shoots are usually pruned hard back in the spring to encourage more to form in the coming year. Although it is true to say that these are normally cut right down almost to the base of the shoots, it is often more interesting to do this on a two-yearly basis. Instead of cutting down every shoot, leave half of them. This allows them to carry on growing to a greater height for a further year, after which they, too, are cut down. The second year's growth is usually just as colorful as the first and you have the advantage of the extra height. This is very much a personal choice and you have to want the taller plants, but it is especially good in a windy position, where the plants provide quite a bit of shelter and protection to other plants, as well as providing an attractive display. You would probably only do this with the shorter species; something like elder *(Sambucus)* might be too vigorous.

1 The way to produce the best foliage on certain shrubs is to prune them severely in mid-spring, as growth starts. This elder bush (Sambucus) is ready to be pruned hard back.

Variegated foliage

1 With golden or variegated shrubs, it is vital to remove any shoots that revert to the normal green color. These will soon dominate the bush if allowed to.

2 In the case of this plant, you should shorten the shoot on the right to give the bush a better balance. If this is done early on, you will hardly notice its removal.

Left: A fine example of a golden foliaged shrub that also bears attractive and complementary flowers. Spiraea x bumalda (japonica) 'Goldflame' flowers after midsummer and is best pruned fairly hard in early to mid-spring to keep it compact and shapely.

2 *Cut back the branches to suitably placed buds; here, they are already breaking into growth. Be very careful not to damage the buds on pruned shoots; there may be no 'spares'.*

Left: *The result of hard pruning is superb young foliage on the strong, one-year-old shoots of this attractive variegated form of Sambucus racemosa.*

Right: *Sambucus racemosa 'Plumosa Aurea' has finely cut yellow foliage and responds well to hard pruning in spring. It produces red berries instead of the usual black ones, but only on the older shoots.*

COLORED STEMS

Some of the shrubs with the most attractive winter stems are found among the dogwoods (Cornus) and willows (Salix).

Varieties of Cornus alba bear plain or variegated foliage through the summer, with attractive fall tints before the bare stems glow in winter.

Right: *The gorgeous red stems of Cornus alba 'Sibirica' will cheer up a colorless corner for the whole winter. Cut them to the ground in mid-spring.*

1 *Cut the stems back in spring, although you can leave some for two years.*

2 *The plant will respond by sending up fresh new shoots that will provide interest through the winter.*

Bush roses

With the exception of rambler roses, which are pruned after they have finished flowering in summer, most roses, including hybrid teas and floribundas, are best lightly pruned in early winter and properly pruned in mid-spring. Lightly pruned bushes can rest in winter and will not rock about in stormy conditions. If a hole were to develop in the soil around the neck of the bush, it could fill with water and start a rot in the bark. (Do not, however, prune roses grown for their decorative hips.) After a mild winter, growth can start in early spring and you cannot bank on the early growth surviving. That is why it is best to delay the second pruning until the worst of the winter is over. Hybrid teas and floribundas are pruned in almost exactly the same way. The only real difference is the severity. The floribundas are not pruned as hard as the teas because the aim is a good display of many flowers, whereas the teas should have fewer but larger blooms. The length to which you cut back the individual shoots in spring will depend on their vigor. Cut back strong hybrid tea bushes to about 12in(30cm) high. Cutting them almost to the ground is going too far, unless they are being grown specifically for show. The extra hard pruning makes them produce later but larger flowers. For ordinary garden flowering, it is better to have the flowers earlier and more of them.

Spring pruning

In spring, first tackle any shoots that are clearly in the wrong place or causing overcrowding. Add to these any that are too weak and feeble to carry decent flowers. Cut both kinds right out or shorten them to a strong bud pointing in the appropriate direction. Cut back the strong shoots on floribundas to about 18in(45cm) long.

Below: *Cut to just above a bud using a sharp pair of secateurs to avoid damaging the stem.*

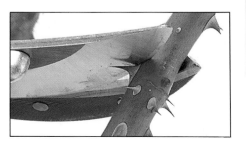

Fall pruning

It is important to prune rose bushes lightly in the fall. This enables the plants to rest in winter, prevents them rocking about in wet, windy weather and tidies up both the plants and the borders. Do not prune them any harder than is necessary. Remove all flowers, buds and hips, and cut back any long shoots by about a third of their length (those taller than 24in/ 60cm). Remove broken and out-of-place shoots. This is not a proper pruning, just an opportunity to make the bushes smaller and tidier.

1 *A hybrid tea rose bush in early winter. Cut back the long shoot to leave it about 24in(60cm) long.*

1 *Cut all dead branches back to their point of origin. Use loppers or a saw if the branches are very thick.*

2 *Remove any dead stems or branches left over after the light pruning given to the plant in the fall.*

2 *Cut out branches carrying hips. They take energy from the plant, so remove them before the winter.*

3 *This is the bush after fall pruning. You could remove the dead growth, but this is not crucial.*

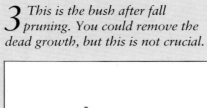

Above: Rosa 'Loving Memory'. A combination of the correct pruning at the right time of year and good management results in a perfect rose.

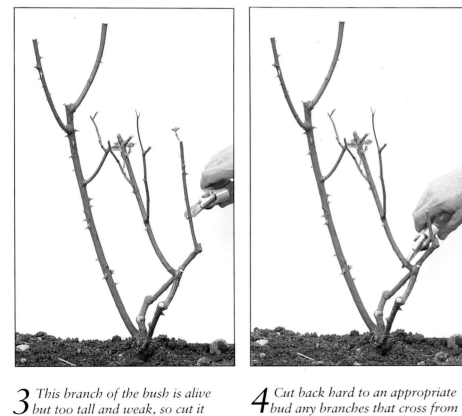

3 *This branch of the bush is alive but too tall and weak, so cut it back to an outward-pointing bud.*

4 *Cut back hard to an appropriate bud any branches that cross from one side of the bush to the other.*

5 *Cut back this tall branch by about half its length to a bud pointing in the direction that you want it to grow.*

6 *Hybrid tea roses need this treatment to perform at their best. Prune floribunda roses more lightly.*

Pruning shrub roses

Although the term 'shrub rose' is a fairly loose one, it refers to those roses that are neither hybrid tea or floribunda (bedding roses), climbing or rambling, nor the miniatures or ground cover roses. This leaves the specie roses, such as *Rosa damascena* and *R. rubrifolia*, all the old-fashioned varieties, such as *Rosa centifolia* and *R. gallica*, the moss roses and English Roses. They are called 'shrub roses' because they are grown like - and look more like - shrubs than conventional rose bushes. Like bedding roses, they are pruned during the summer but, like many late-flowering shrubs, they are also tidied up in the fall. Not all roses are late-flowering; a great many of the rose species flower in the spring and early summer on the previous year's shoots, such as the spectacular 'Canary Bird'. Like other flowering shrubs, the shrub roses are largely pruned according to when they flower; early ones after flowering; later ones in the spring as growth starts. However, there is one important exception to this general rule: roses that are grown as much for their ornamental hips as for their flowers are pruned in spring to allow their hips to develop fully and stay on the bushes as long as possible. *Rosa rugosa* and *R. moyesii* 'Geranium' are well-known for their hips. As with many flowering shrubs, the aim of pruning is to keep bushes young, by removing old and worn out branch systems and by shortening back any over-vigorous young shoots. Try to maintain a full, but not overcrowded, young plant. Deadhead those plants that you are not saving for their hips.

Right: 'Cardinal de Richelieu', one of the oldest and best gallica roses, needs quite hard pruning to maintain flower size. Remove the oldest branches in spring but leave vigorous young shoots entire.

Summer pruning

1 *This favorite old-fashioned moss rose, 'William Lobb', is being deadheaded a bit later than it should have been. The hips are well developed and have already set seed.*

2 *When deadheading, always cut back to a bud or a shoot growing in the direction you want. With early-flowering roses, this form of pruning might well lead to more blooms.*

Deadheading

The reason for removing the dead flowers from roses and other flowering shrubs is that, if they are left to form seed, the bush virtually stops flowering. the process of seed formation is sometimes said to 'wear out' the bush, but the real reason is simpler. Once seed has formed, the job is to build and ripen it, not produce flowers.

Above: *It is better to remove a poor new shoot completely and cut hard back to a suitably strong bud further down.*

Left: *Prune* Rosa rugosa *lightly in spring. If you dead head the flowers, you will also lose the beautiful hips.*

Above: *This 'Canary Bird' is just past its best. It would be impossible to remove all the dead flowers so leave it alone to grow and form naturally. Any hips that appear can be cut off later.*

WINTER/SPRING PRUNING

To keep the bush young and flowering strongly, cut back older sections of a branch to a young growth. If necessary, cut out a complete branch system.

Cut out all weak growths completely. They will never make strong flowering shoots and could prevent new ones from forming,

Cut back whole sections of flowered stems to a strong bud, especially if other young shoots are plentiful.

3 *'William Lobb' does not usually produce many more flowers, but other varieties will do so. Summer pruning coupled with deadheading is a good habit to adopt and it also tidies up the bush.*

Climbing and rambler roses

The strategies for pruning climbing and rambler roses are very different. Climbers are normally vigorous growers and often sports (mutations) of hybrid teas or floribundas. In the early years they are pruned to encourage them to grow quickly and cover the area allotted to them. Later, the aim is to create a good balance between growth and flowering. Much of the framework of branches stays, because the best flowers are found on the vigorous shoots growing from them. Tie them in as they grow to stop them waving about.

Ramblers work on a different system, because the long and vigorous shoots grow one year and flower the next, after which they are pruned fairly radically. For this reason, they need training in a different way to climbers. The most convenient way is to tie them over arches or along pergolas. After flowering, towards the end of summer, untie them from their supports and spread them out on the ground so that you can see what is going on. Identify the long shoots that have flowered and either cut them out completely or shorten them to a vigorous shoot of the current year's growth arising from near their base. Which you do depends on the total number of new shoots, remembering that it is these that will flower the following summer. If there are many, cut out the flowered shoots completely. If they are scarce, then cut back a certain number of the old shoots to strong side shoots.

Above: *Classifying a rose is not always easy. 'Pompon de Paris', is described as a weak (compact) climber and must be pruned accordingly.*

Climbing or rambler rose?

It is important to know which kind of rose - climber or rambler - you are pruning. If you treat them the same, one will flourish and the other will be something of a failure. In their young state, when you buy them, they look very similar, so ask the nursery which kind they are. If in doubt, check the name and habit in a reliable reference book. If you buy a young climber during the dormant winter season, prune it quite hard after planting. This encourages strong new shoots that you tie to the wall or fence. If a new rambler has a few strong, young shoots, keep them, but cut all the others right out.

Left: *If a rambler has been properly pruned and trained after flowering, it will look neat and tidy throughout the winter. In very cold spells, you can tie the stems more closely together for mutual protection.*

Right: *A blaze of summer color is the reward for correct and timely pruning and training. Ramblers have just one flush of flowers but this can last for several weeks and is often spectacular.*

Pruning an established climber

1 This naturally weak climber does not produce many new shoots each summer. Keep some of the older ones, shortened, for another year.

2 Cut out weak and spindly growth and shorten the side shoots that carried the flowers hard back. Also shorten overly long new shoots.

Above: 'American Pillar' used to be a more popular rambler, but its color does not appeal to everyone. The rather stiff growth also makes it tricky to train, but it flowers profusely.

3 Creating stress on the branches by bending them over in an arched fashion persuades climbing plants to produce the maximum amount of flower and to shoot from the base. Use soft natural string.

4 With all the pruning done, the bush looks much tidier and has been spread out and tied back to the supporting wires.

Climbing plants

In contrast to wall shrubs, climbers have the means to hang on to a support with little or no help. They might twine around other plants, as honeysuckle does, hang on with tendrils, like clematis, or it have aerial roots or 'suckers', like ivy. Climbing and rambler roses and the blackberry family climb by using their thorns. Without anything to climb up, all these plants would collapse. In gardens, most climbers need a little help at first; once started off, they carry on by themselves. There are also what might be called 'scramblers', such as winter jasmine and periwinkle. These will clamber up a support, but will run along the ground if not trained and secured. How you prune and train climbers depends on the plant in question. Annuals and those perennials that die down every winter can often be left to their own devices; merely point them in the right direction when they appear to be straying from it. Twiggy sticks are quite suitable for the shorter climbers of this kind, such as sweet peas, which have tendrils for hanging on. The more vigorous ones, such as the ornamental hop, will be happier to twine up rough string.

Late-flowering clematis

1 Clematis that bloom from midsummer onwards, flower on shoots that grew earlier in the same growing season. Prune them in early spring after the first signs of growth.

Honeysuckle

1 If a new honeysuckle is to cover a wall or fence, untwine the shoots from the cane and train them over the supporting frame.

2 Tie the shoots to the support rather than twine them back and forth through the trellis. The twining can easily strip buds off the shoots.

3 A fairly hard first pruning enables the plant to build up a strong framework with plenty of radial shoots. Always cut back to a live bud.

4 A young honeysuckle that has been pruned back quite hard after planting grows away well and soon covers the area allocated to it.

Below: Lonicera x tellmanniana, *a hybrid between an American and Chinese honeysuckle, bears attractive, but unscented, apricot yellow flowers.*

Above: Clematis 'Nelly Moser', one of the most popular large-flowered, mid- to late summer-flowering hybrids. Pruned in spring, as shown on these pages, it will provide a reliable show of flowers.

4 Many gardeners pruning late-flowering clematis for the first time are anxious that the severe treatment will kill the plant, but this is how it should look when you have finished.

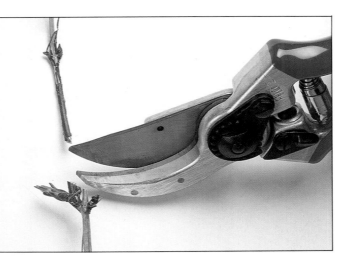

2 You need not prune back every shoot every year, but any that are left will carry on growing before they flower. This could result in flowers 10ft(3m) or more above ground level.

3 Always cut back to a live bud to avoid leaving unsightly snags that may become infected by fungal diseases. The direction in which the bud is facing is of no importance.

Pruning hops and other herbaceous climbers

1 Leaving the dead stems until spring gives the crown of the plant some winter protection, but for tidiness you may prefer to cut down the tops in early winter after they die.

2 Leave just 2in(5cm) or so of the stalks to show you where the plant is. This saves you chopping it to pieces with a hoe when you work the ground any time after cutting back the tops.

Below: The 'golden hop', an eye-catching and vigorous climber, will soon cover a shed. Being perennial, it is killed to the ground by frost; remember this when siting it.

Above: Clematis 'Bill Mackenzie' needs little pruning. If necessary, cut it back quite hard in spring, even though you may lose a year's flowers.

Above: Only prune Clematis montana when it has outgrown its position. Then, in spring, pull it down, cut back dead and young shoots and retrain the older wood; new shoots soon grow.

Pruning clematis

Those flowering in spring or early summer do so on the previous year's shoots. If needed, prune them after flowering. Prune hybrids, and others that flower after about midsummer, in spring as growth starts. They flower best on the current season's growth, so cut them to within 1-2ft (30-60cm) of the ground. If not pruned, the flowers appear higher each year.

Climbing strategies

TWINERS
Actinidia kolomikta
Aristolochia *(calico flower)*
Campsis *(trumpet vine)*
Fallopia baldschuanica
Humulus lupulus *(hop)*
Lonicera *(honeysuckle)*
Trachelospermum jasminoides
Wisteria

TENDRILS & LEAF STALKS
Clematis
Eccremocarpus *(glory vine)*
Passiflora *(passion flower)*
Vitis *(grape vines and others)*

PADS & GRIPPING ROOTS
Hedera *(ivy)*
Hydrangea petiolaris
Parthenocissus *(Virginia creeper)*

THORNS
Rubus *(blackberries, brambles)*
Rosa *(climbing & rambler roses)*

LOOSE CLIMBERS
Abutilon megapotamicum
Chaenomeles *(flowering quince)*
Forsythia suspensa
Jasminum *(summer & winter)*
Solanum crispum

Wisteria

Below: *Ivy is one of the best self-clinging climbers. It needs very little regular pruning, but remove green shoots from variegated varieties.*

Above: *Prune outdoor varieties of the passion flower, (Passiflora), hard every spring. Wait until new shoots appear. Do not prune to a dormant bud.*

Below: *Once established, cut back new wisteria growth to 6in(15cm) in midsummer and, further, to 2in(5cm) in winter. This encourages flowering spurs to form instead of just new shoots.*

Below: *In early summer, Wisteria floribunda 'Rosea' produces masses of strongly scented, pale purple-pink flowers. It is clear that the panicles are made up of pealike flowers; in fact, wisteria belongs to the pea family.*

Wall shrubs

There are two definitions of a wall shrub. It is either any shrub that is not a climber but which is planted against a wall for support, or it is a shrub on the borderline of hardiness that is grown against or close to a wall for protection from the weather. In the first category you find a few shrubs, such as *Cotoneaster horizontalis*, which, in spite of its name, looks very attractive when grown against a wall instead of on the flat. *Forsythia suspensa* and winter jasmine could also be included in this category. Because these plants, and others like them, are perfectly hardy, a wooden fence would serve as well as a wall. However, true wall shrubs form quite a large group of plants that actually need the extra warmth or shelter from cold winds that a wall provides. A house wall that receives the sun at midday faces the sun for a long time and is sheltered from cold winds. The brick-work also warms up and it is the heat given off by a wall at night that can be just as beneficial to the plants growing near to or against it. Thus, a warm, sunny wall is an excellent place for early-flowering shrubs and small trees, including fruits such as peaches and nectarines, that are perfectly hardy in other respects. The warmth stops the flowers being frosted and killed. Because you could be dealing with many different kinds, shapes and sizes of shrubs, there is no one training system that does for all. However, you can use the wall to advantage by making it a form of support for trees and shrubs that, in a warmer climate, would be fully in the open. By training them to a warm wall, you are showing them off better, as well as giving them more favorable growing conditions. The prime example of this is the glorious *Fremontodendron* 'Californian Glory', which needs the warmth of a house wall and is seen at its best when trained fairly formally against it. The questionably hardy *Garrya elliptica*, the tassel bush, is different because it is definitely best grown freely and unimpeded. This lovely shrub does best tucked into a warm corner. To complete the picture, fuchsias and *Lavatera* 'Barnsley', both semi-hardy, can be pruned less severely if they are protected from frosts.

Pyracantha

2 *Tie the central stem to one of the vertical members of the frame with soft string. This plant is intended to grow informally against its support.*

1 *Choose the best side shoots and train them along the trellis panel. Cut back any shoots growing straight towards or away from the frame.*

3 *Tie in any side shoots so that they point in the right direction. Do not tie them horizontally, as this looks too formal and reduces the plant's vigor.*

Right: *Pyracantha makes a lovely sight when trained to a wall and carrying its familiar berries. You can train it either formally, with the branches spreading out horizontally from the central stem, or informally, with much less regimentation, as shown here.*

4 Tied to the frame like this, all the retained shoots form the basis of a larger plant that will cover the trellis completely in three to four years.

Forsythia

Although you would not normally grow *Forsythia x intermedia* against a wall, it makes an excellent subject, flowers earlier and represents many shrubs that can be similarly treated.

1 Plant the forsythia about 6in (15cm) away from the support. Tie in the stems loosely with string or plastic-covered wire. A tight tie will soon bite into the vigorous shoots.

2 Tie in the main shoots (here there are four), so that they cover a wide area of the frame. Cut out any weak, out-of-place shoots, together with any branches that are clearly not needed.

3 Cut away any shoots that are growing straight out from the plant, as they will not be suitable for bending back towards the frame later on.

4 Lightly cut back the remaining branches to encourage side shoots. With shrubs that flower in spring, you need plenty of new growth to produce abundant flowers the following year.

5 With all the shoots tied in and shortened, all they need is the warmth of spring to start them into growth. Do not allow young shrubs to flower too much at this tender age or growth will suffer and the plant will take longer to cover the frame.

Wall supports

 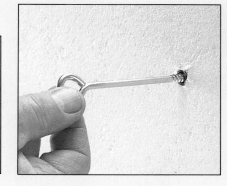 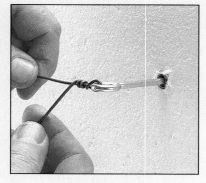

1 Drill a hole for the wall support. This is much better than knocking in the eye with a hammer, as there is no risk of splitting. Short cuts don't work!

2 After pushing in a wall plug, screw in the screw-eye, leaving the eye about 2in(5cm) out from the wall. This allows room for tying shoots to the wire.

3 Pass one end of the wire through the eye and twist it around itself several times. This is another reason for keeping the wire away from the wall.

Below: Fremontodendron 'Californian Glory' is one of the most rewarding wall shrubs, but not fully hardy in colder areas. It needs the extra heat provided by a sunny wall to survive.

Vine eyes

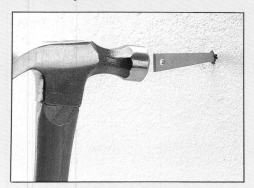

1 To stop the wire sagging or coming away, drive in vine eyes every 6ft (1.8m). Draw the wire across to the next screw eye to give a straight line.

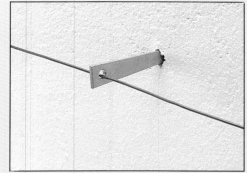

2 Only attach the far end of the wire temporarily; once the vine eyes have been driven in, it will have to be detached and passed through each eye.

Left: Most Ceanothus benefit not only from the extra warmth of a sunny wall, but also from its support. Tying the shrub to horizontal wires is the most effective way because it can be made to cover quite a large area.

Right: Garrya elliptica needs the greater warmth of a wall, as severe winter weather can damage both the foliage and the tassels. This specimen is trained to a wall, but it will also grow free-standing in a sunny corner.

Right: *Most people think of Cotoneaster* horizontalis *as a scrambling, ground cover shrub. Although fully hardy, it can be even more effective when trained to a wall or fence. It shows up the interesting 'herringbone' habit much more clearly.*

Above: *Ribes* speciosum *is not grown as much as it should be. It makes an excellent wall shrub, where the early flowers are also protected from frost.*

Left: *The unusual flowers of Ribes* speciosum *show up beautifully against a brick wall. When grown as a free-standing bush, the flowers hang down from the low-growing branches and are largely hidden by the foliage.*

Wall shrubs that need protection

Abelia
Abutilon *
Aloysia *(Lemon verbena)*
Callistemon (Bottlebrush) *
Camellia
Ceanothus
Chimonanthus
Corokia
Crinodendron *(Lantern tree)* *
Cytisus battandieri
Eriobotrya *(Loquat)* *
Escallonia
Eucryphia
Fabiana
Fremontodendron
Garrya elliptica *(Tassel bush)*

Grevillea *
Hamamelis *(Witch hazel)*
Hebe
Hibiscus
Indigofera
Leptospermum *
Magnolia
Myrtus *(Myrtle)*
Phlomis *(Jerusalem sage)*
Pittosporum
Punica *(Pomegranate)* *
Teucrium

* *These shrubs are more tender and usually need extra protection during the winter months.*

Heathers and other ground cover plants

One of the virtues of ground cover plants is their ability, once established, to smother weeds. Always prepare the ground well before planting, digging out any weeds, especially perennials, such as dock and bindweed. Choose plants with a naturally low-growing, spreading habit that grow fairly quickly, and fill any gaps with some of the creeping annuals, such as nasturtium, until the permanent plants have grown. Put in bold groups of the same plants rather than many different ones and plant subjects of near equal vigor. In the early years, pruning and training go hand in hand; the aim is to encourage plants to spread as quickly as possible, ruthlessly curbing any excessive upward growth. This means bending and pegging it to the ground to reduce the height and increase the sideways spread. At this stage, training normally takes precedence over pruning. To restore a mature area of ground cover plants to its youthful vigor, tackle it in the spring as growth is starting; new growth will quickly arise from old wood.

Ceratostigma

When the buds start opening in the spring, cut back the flowered shoots to living wood. This may mean cutting out whole shoots.

Below: This useful plant is not reliably hardy and often suffers dieback in a severe winter.

Heathers

Heathers, such as Erica carnea 'Myreton Ruby', shown below, are highly effective ground cover plants, but they only thrive in acid soil. As they are quite slow-growing, do not plant them with vigorous companions that will quickly smother them.

Below: While heathers are young and recently planted, grasp each plant by the spent flower heads and simply clip off the handful with secateurs.

Above: Once the bed is established, wait until flowering is over, then clip back the old blooms with shears and tidy up the plants. This will encourage strong growth for the next season.

Hebe

Old specimens of hebe become leggy and bare on the inside, but it is possible to rejuvenate them by cutting them hard back. The results may not look exciting, but the plants soon recover.

Right: Hebe pagei. *This dwarf hebe responds well to hard pruning, but is not long-lived.*

1 This old hebe is starting to put out fresh growth from the base. Cut back the plant to these new shoots in the spring to encourage even more healthy new growths to develop.

2 By the end of the current growing season, you will be rewarded with quite a lot of new growth. Pull up or hoe any weeds that might appear on the bare ground as you see them.

Hypericum

Cut ground cover hypericum hard back to within 1in(2.5cm) of the ground to stop this invasive plant becoming leggy and spreading too far. Normally, you would prune every spring, but good results are also possible by cutting in alternate springs.

Right: Hypericum calycinum *is a magnificent plant for covering the ground and smothering out weeds in the border.*

Vinca

Vinca major *and* V. minor *are ground cover favorites. Shoot tips root readily and send up fresh clumps.* V. major *is highly invasive; plant it where there is a wall on one side and grass (and therefore a mower) on the other to keep it in control. Both species flower well,* V. minor *in a range of colors.*

Above: Vinca minor *'Bowles' Blue' is less vigorous than Vinca major. Cut it back with greater care.*

1 This is what happens to V. major *after a few years of vigorous growth. It will flower well and is even more effective at choking out weeds, but there is rather too much of it to be attractive.*

2 Plenty of young shoots break out the whole time to add to the tangled mass. Cutting back to these shoots in the spring will rejuvenate the plant. Pruning every other year or one in three will be enough.

3 With all the old and leafless stems cut away, the result is a new patch of periwinkles. Within a very weeks the new shoots will be growing away strongly and the ground will soon be covered again.

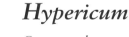

The principles of pruning fruit

It goes without saying that we grow fruit trees and bushes to produce fruit. However, it is the earlier stage - flowering - that is influenced by pruning. The first thing to remember is that a fruit tree or bush will fruit tolerably well if it is not pruned at all. After all, this is what happens in the wild. Any pruning that we do, therefore, must be aimed at improving flowering and hence, fruiting. This may sound simple, but you need to know what you are doing before you can judge its effect. The next point is that, certainly with tree fruits, a vertical branch tends to grow at the expense of fruiting. If you cut back the tall shoots at the top of large fruit trees, they immediately grow more strongly and rigidly. However, if you allow them to fruit, the weight of the crop will bend them over and growth is dramatically reduced. On the other hand, a horizontal branch fruits at the expense of growth. This is clear to see in espalier-trained apple and pear trees, where the cropping branches are in horizontal pairs on either side of a vertical central stem. In fact, for their first year or two, the young branches are trained more upright, as they would take too long to grow out horizontally. The final point is that there must be a reason for every pruning cut you make. No snipping about in complete ignorance; it can do more harm than good. Bear these thoughts in mind and you are halfway towards understanding pruning.

Above: Apples and pears are normally pruned in winter when they are dormant. You should finish pruning before the developing shoots reach the 'mouse-ear' stage shown here.

Buds on a fruit tree

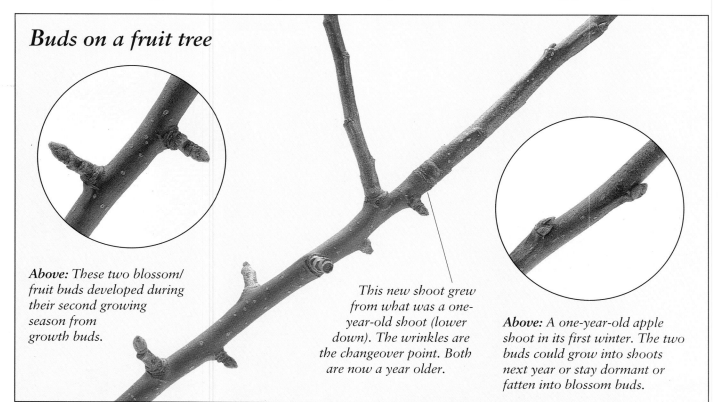

Above: These two blossom/fruit buds developed during their second growing season from growth buds.

This new shoot grew from what was a one-year-old shoot (lower down). The wrinkles are the changeover point. Both are now a year older.

Above: A one-year-old apple shoot in its first winter. The two buds could grow into shoots next year or stay dormant or fatten into blossom buds.

Spur-bearing and tip-bearing varieties

Apple varieties vary in that some carry most of their fruit on spurs while others carry much of it on the tips of short shoots.

70

NOTCHING AND NICKING TO INFLUENCE THE DEVELOPMENT OF A BUD

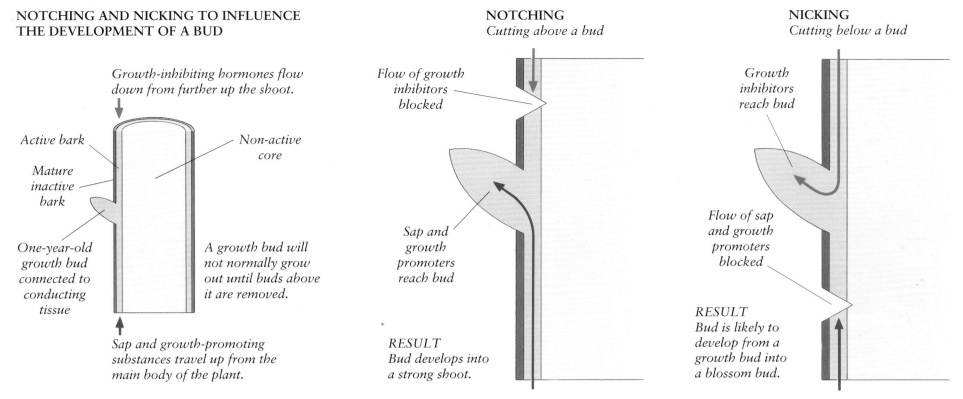

Growth-inhibiting hormones flow down from further up the shoot.

Active bark

Mature inactive bark

Non-active core

One-year-old growth bud connected to conducting tissue

A growth bud will not normally grow out until buds above it are removed.

Sap and growth-promoting substances travel up from the main body of the plant.

NOTCHING
Cutting above a bud

Flow of growth inhibitors blocked

Sap and growth promoters reach bud

RESULT
Bud develops into a strong shoot.

NICKING
Cutting below a bud

Growth inhibitors reach bud

Flow of sap and growth promoters blocked

RESULT
Bud is likely to develop from a growth bud into a blossom bud.

Notching a plant to create shoot growth

A few apple varieties carry much of their fruit on the end of small shoots (shown above) and the rest on spurs. Each of the 'spur' systems, or 'fruiting spurs', shown left, developed from a single fruit bud that carried fruit. Simplify overcrowded spurs to improve the quality of the fruit.

1 When notching a growth bud to make it grow out, cut the notch 0.4in(1cm) above the bud. This has the maximum effect on the bud. Carry out this procedure in winter.

2 Be sure to make the notch so that it goes right through the bark but only just into the wood underneath. A small wound of this size will heal by the fall and cause no lasting damage.

3 The completed notch. The effect of this and of nicking below a growth bud is extremely quick and you can expect to see results soon after growth starts in the spring.

Shaping a bush tree

1 *To shape a normal 'bush tree', select and retain four or five suitable shoots as the future main branches. Start by shortening them by one third to half their length.*

2 *The result of these early stages of pruning is a well-shaped and balanced tree that will produce a strong framework of branches able to carry good crops of healthy apples.*

Only cut out those branches that are rubbing or causing over-crowding. Harmless ones can be left to fruit.

3 *By midsummer, the young tree has produced many more shoots. Leave them until the winter, when you can carry out the appropriate pruning to encourage more branches.*

Half-standard and bush fruit trees

At one time, nearly all fruit trees were 'standards'. This means that they were far too big for an average garden, with trunks some 6ft(1.8m) tall. Standard trees have largely disappeared now and have been replaced by half-standards with 4ft(1.2m) tall trunks and bush trees with 30in(75cm) trunks. Smaller trees are available, but they are really for enthusiasts and experienced gardeners. For everyday gardens and gardeners where 'fruit without tears' is required, half-standards and bush are the answer. Although bush trees are smaller, they are not always the most convenient in gardens. A trunk measuring only 30in(75cm) tall is very difficult to work and mow under. The lowest branches are far too near the ground for convenience. Half-standards, on the other hand, have plenty of room under them both for cultivating and mowing and are much more convenient. If you have difficulty in finding one, choose a one-year-old (maiden) whip and allow the trunk to grow until it is 5ft(1.5m) tall. Then prune out the top so that the lowest side shoot is about 4ft(1.2m) from the ground.

Right: Spindlebush trees have a central stem with fruiting side shoots. You can stop the stem at any convenient height; 7ft(2.1m) is right for most people.

Regulated pruning

Renewal pruning

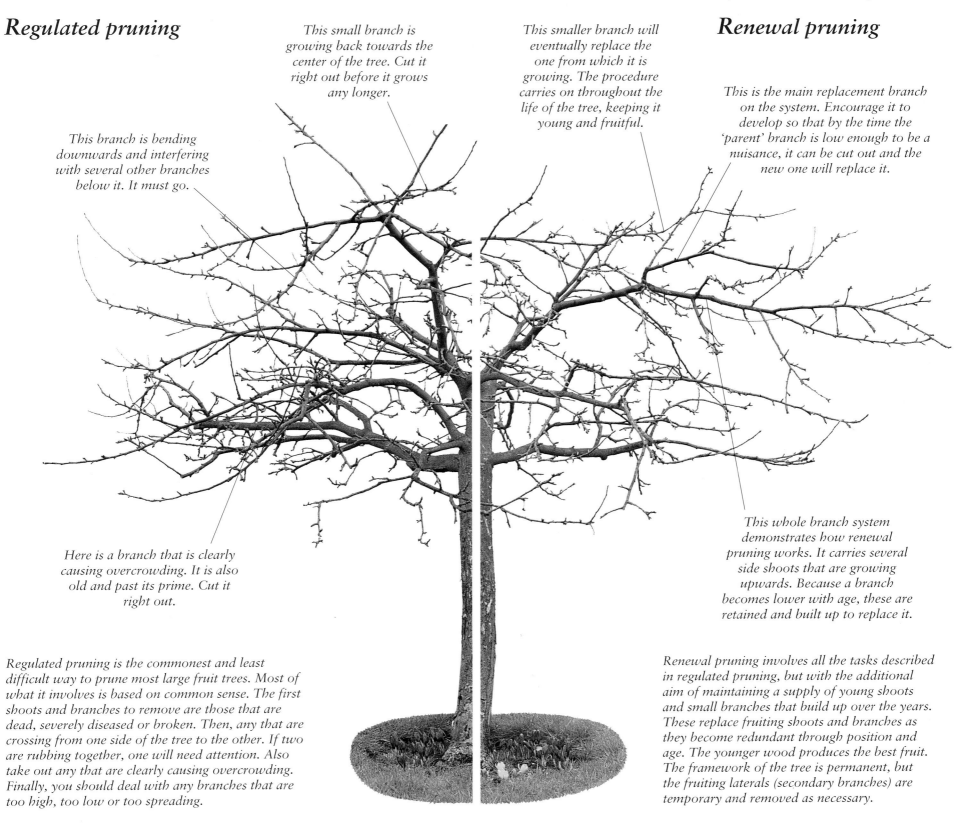

This small branch is growing back towards the center of the tree. Cut it right out before it grows any longer.

This smaller branch will eventually replace the one from which it is growing. The procedure carries on throughout the life of the tree, keeping it young and fruitful.

This is the main replacement branch on the system. Encourage it to develop so that by the time the 'parent' branch is low enough to be a nuisance, it can be cut out and the new one will replace it.

This branch is bending downwards and interfering with several other branches below it. It must go.

Here is a branch that is clearly causing overcrowding. It is also old and past its prime. Cut it right out.

This whole branch system demonstrates how renewal pruning works. It carries several side shoots that are growing upwards. Because a branch becomes lower with age, these are retained and built up to replace it.

Regulated pruning is the commonest and least difficult way to prune most large fruit trees. Most of what it involves is based on common sense. The first shoots and branches to remove are those that are dead, severely diseased or broken. Then, any that are crossing from one side of the tree to the other. If two are rubbing together, one will need attention. Also take out any that are clearly causing overcrowding. Finally, you should deal with any branches that are too high, too low or too spreading.

Renewal pruning involves all the tasks described in regulated pruning, but with the additional aim of maintaining a supply of young shoots and small branches that build up over the years. These replace fruiting shoots and branches as they become redundant through position and age. The younger wood produces the best fruit. The framework of the tree is permanent, but the fruiting laterals (secondary branches) are temporary and removed as necessary.

Cordons and espaliers

The cordon is the simplest way of training apple and pear trees intensively. Once you have the principle under control, you can create many interesting and fruitful shapes. Cordons are best planted and trained at a 45° angle to reduce their vigor and encourage fruiting. Cut back any side shoots that are present at planting to three buds straight afterwards. When side shoots appear in subsequent years, prune them in the same way but in late summer. After that, when shoots grow from those already pruned back, shorten the new ones in late summer back to one bud. Summer pruning encourages fruit buds and fruiting spurs to form. The espalier is really just a vertical cordon but with pairs of horizontal branches 10-12in (25-30cm) apart. Espaliers are trained to wires and can be grown against a wall or in the open. You can form an espalier either by training out a tier of branches to their full length before going up to the next or by starting a fresh tier every year and developing them all together. To grow a tier a year, start with a single-stemmed tree with no side shoots and cut it back to a bud just above and pointing out from the bottom wire. The next two buds down will form the first tier of horizontal branches and the top bud will extend the stem upwards. From then on, do the same every winter until the tree is as tall as you want.

Above: *Step-over trees make good edging plants for the side of vegetable plots or they can be dividers between sections of garden. They are both ornamental and fruitful.*

Right: *For more ambitious gardeners, an espalier takes longer to form but is the envy of neighbors and carries good crops after just a few years. The modern apple 'Greensleeves' is ideal.*

Left: Oblique cordons are probably the most space efficient way of growing apples and pears. Most will form fruiting spurs readily and you can grow many trees in a small space.

Below: You can grow cordons in the open garden against a wire and cane support or, as here, against a fence or wall. Pears thrive on a sunny wall, where the fruits ripen to perfection.

Pruning cordon fruit trees

Although cordon and espalier apples and pears are best pruned in late summer, these photographs show winter pruning for clarity. The procedure in summer is very simple. Cut back new shoots growing direct from main stems or branches to 3in(7.5cm) long at a leaf and those from existing spurs to 1in(2.5cm) long.

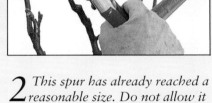

1 *This is a cordon in winter ready for pruning. Postpone this job until the leaves have fallen so you can see just what you are doing.*

2 *This spur has already reached a reasonable size. Do not allow it to grow any larger, so cut back the extension growth to a fruit bud.*

3 *As in summer pruning, prune new shoots from main stems to 3in(7.5cm), and those from spurs pruned earlier to 1in(2.5cm).*

Right: The tree in summer shortly before you would prune it. It is carrying a promising crop, but do not carry out fruit thinning until after the natural fruit drop in midsummer.

1 Only if you are very lucky will you find a young tree in the nursery as well-shaped as this one. It is perfect for fan-training. Most other trees, though, can be modified by retaining only those 'branches' growing in the same plane.

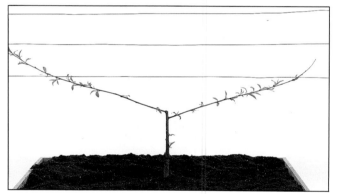

2 Taking your courage in both hands, cut back the young tree to leave just two suitable shoots to form the first rays of the fan. It does not leave much, but it is the best way to start training the plant.

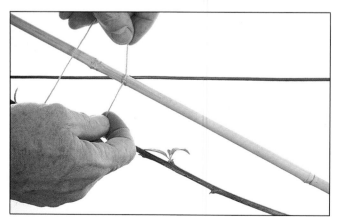

3 The permanent wires are 9-12in (23-30cm) apart. Tie two primary training canes to the wires. Use plastic string for the canes, as it lasts longer.

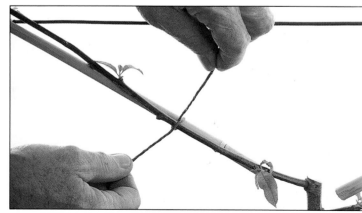

4 Tie the shoots to the canes, but not too tightly to avoid strangling the developing shoots. Use soft string, not plastic, for the same reason.

Training a peach tree to wires

As peaches and nectarines are natives of the Mediterranean, they can seldom be grown as free-standing trees in the open garden in cooler, temperate countries. There, they need the protection of a warm and sunny wall or fence to give of their best. Fan-trained trees are undoubtedly the most successful in this situation and training against a wall is always better than a fence because the brickwork holds a lot more heat. This is released at night and will frequently raise the temperature around the tree sufficiently to keep away a light frost. Fan-trained trees are better than espaliers, because peach branches are not always long-lived and may die back from time to time. If this happens on an espalier, it can take several years for a replacement to grow, develop and fruit, whereas with a fan, the 'spokes' are simply closed up to fill the gap and replacements are being trained outwards the whole time. When training a tree in a fan shape, carry out the work as well as you can, because what is done in the early years has a great influence on the tree's future. Peaches and nectarines are grown in exactly the same way; the nectarine is simply a hairless 'sport' (mutant) of the peach. 'Peach leaf curl' is a crippling and disfiguring fungus disease that causes first the young leaves and then the older ones to become blistered, swollen and bright red. Complete control is almost impossible but covering the trees with plastic when it rains during the growing season keeps the leaves dry and greatly reduces the spread of this fungus.

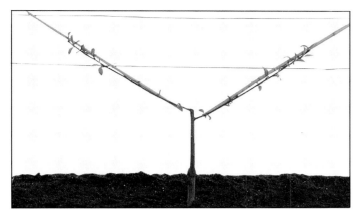

5 In spring the peach tree begins to come to life again and starts to send out new shoots from the original two branches that were retained and tied in to the wires.

6 This is how the tree is looking by midsummer. The righthand side is more vigorous than the left but this does not matter; the unevenness can be corrected later by further training.

7 Tie in new canes as the tree grows; this is the first of several that will be added. It will support the lowest shoot and is temporarily tied to the stem of the tree to hold it in position.

8 It does not matter whether a new shoot is on the upper or lower surface of the branch. If there is a gap in the fan that needs filling, use the nearest and most suitable shoot.

Add more wires to the wall as the tree grows and needs them.

9 This new cane has been added for a shoot growing from the upper surface of the branch. Although it is still summer, the tree has almost finished its first season. There will be little fresh growth from now on.

10 Here is the tree flowering in the following spring. Since you cannot be sure how many side shoots a young tree will develop, leave all the buds to grow into shoots until this time.

The fruiting stage

When the tree has reached this stage, you must start to think of fruiting as well as growth. From now on, they are of equal importance; continue to build up the tree but at the same time consider the development of side shoots for carrying the fruit. The one factor above all others that you must remember is that peaches and nectarines only fruit on the shoots that grew the *previous* year. They are the only tree fruits that normally do this. Bear this in mind when pruning; even if a young shoot appears to be in the wrong place, you can often leave it there for just one more year so that it carries fruit. After that, you can cut it out. You must also remember to save shoots that are growing out from the base of a fruiting shoot because they will become fruiting shoots in the coming year. In early fall, when the fruit has been picked and you can still see where it came from, cut back nearly all those shoots that have carried the fruit to one or two new shoots that will have formed at the base. Only leave those shoots that are to grow on and either fill up gaps in the fan or replace existing and older shoots. Those are about the only occasions when a fruited shoot is left on the tree. Winter pruning is almost nil. No stone fruit should be pruned during the dormant period for fear of catching 'silver leaf' disease.

3 *During the summer, it has become quite obvious that the most upright branch on the righthand half of the tree is too vigorous and is dominating the whole tree. Now is the time to take drastic action.*

1 *Cut out any unwanted shoots. The one being removed is growing straight out from the branch and can never be bent round and tied in satisfactorily.*

2 *Add more training canes as needed and check older ties for tightness. The righthand side of the tree is still dominant but leave it a bit longer.*

Removing shoots

Early in the growing season, remove shoots about 1in(2.5cm) long, or shorter, embryonic shoots that are clearly growing in the wrong places. These will only have to be cut out later after the tree has wasted energy on them.

4 *The only solution is to remove the greater part of the dominant branch. The side shoot being tied in was growing from near its base and was perfectly positioned to replace it. Still use string ties because many will need replacing before the year is out.*

5 *Cutting out the dominant branch has made a vast improvement to the overall appearance of the tree. And, with all the new growths tied in or cut out, you can see what you are doing. More importantly, the tree is starting to look like a fan.*

Hand pollination

Peaches flower before the pollinating insects are about. So before you count your fruitlets, you will need to pollinate the flowers by hand.

Right: *On a sunny day, gently wipe a soft paintbrush across the face of each flower so that pollen is transferred from the male anthers to the stigma.*

6 *In the following spring, the result of the pruning and training is clear to see. The tree is carrying a good show of blossom and all is looking well for the first proper crop of peaches.*

Left: *If the flowers are pollinated and fertilization took place, and the summer was a good one, the result will be a crop of tasty peaches. This is a peach shoot in early summer after the first thinning of the fruitlets.*

Pruning a new blackcurrant bush

Start with a good-quality, strong-growing bush. This one-year-old example has three vigorous shoots and a good root system. Dig out a hole wide enough to take the root system and deep enough to allow the bush to be planted about 2in(5cm) deeper than it was before.

1 *Having spread out the roots in the planting hole, cover them with soil. Shake the bush so that each root is in contact with the earth. Firm the soil down to prevent it drying out and to support the bush.*

2 *Once the bush is planted, completely remove all the weak shoots and shorten the remainder to two or three buds long.*

3 *This treatment encourages strong shoots to grow from the base. It stimulates the root system, so that the bush establishes quickly.*

Blackcurrants

The aim of pruning blackcurrants is to keep the bushes young and compact. Blackcurrants are usually pruned in early winter by cutting out branch systems when they reach four years old. To keep the bushes small, reduce this to three or even two years. Because the bushes will be smaller, also reduce the planting distance between them in the first place or the crop from a given length of row will be considerably lighter. A simple way to establish the age of a branch is to start with the young shoot at the tip and count backwards down the branch. Each year's growth is darker. Good garden varieties include 'Ben Sarek' and 'Ben Lomond'. 'Ben Connan' is a new blackcurrant variety that is reputed to have the largest individual currants of all and good disease-resistance, too.

Pruning a mature blackcurrant

1 *Cut out all branches that are more than three years old and any growing too close to the ground or across the bush.*

Right: This black-currant bush has just flowered. It has been pruned so that there are no low-growing branches to touch the ground when fruits develop. The bush is not excessively tall because some of the older branch systems have been removed every winter during pruning.

Buds and shoots

Below: A one-year-old blackcurrant shoot. Note the fat fruit buds that will carry fruit next summer. Do not remove a shoot like this.

Below: The central stem of this two-year-old branch fruited in the previous summer and produced the side shoots that will fruit next year. Then you may need to remove it.

Below: 'Ben Sarek' is a relative newcomer among blackcurrants. The bush is significantly smaller than other varieties, yet it is heavy cropping.

2 Tidy the bush by cutting back any growth that extends beyond the space you want the plant to occupy.

3 Cut long shoots right out. Shortening a young shoot encourages growth and branching, which makes it even larger.

Pruning redcurrants

Cultivated not as conventional bushes but as cordons, both redcurrants, and their colorless cousins the whitecurrants, take up very little room and will grow either in the open garden trained to canes or against a wall or fence. U-cordons are more economical of plants than single vertical cordons, but the latter will cover the area more quickly. Prune them in early summer by cutting back the new shoots to within 4in(10cm) of the main branches and, further, to 2in(5cm) in the winter. Summer pruning encourages the currants to grow and ripen and also reduces the amount of soft, sappy growth, which would be susceptible to mildew disease. The Dutch variety 'Jonkheer van Tets' (early) and 'Red Lake' (midseason) are both excellent in gardens. Grow 'Stanza' for a late crop. 'White Versailles' is the most widely grown whitecurrant. Propagate both kinds by hardwood cuttings in early winter. Although mildew is sometimes seen, it is never as serious as it is on gooseberries. One of the modern fungicides should control it. Spray early in the year when the buds are opening and repeat twice at two-week intervals. The worst pests are usually aphids that cause red blisters to form on leaves. If this is serious, any systemic insecticide will control them.

Pruning a new redcurrant

All the formative pruning in the early years is done in winter. Do not carry out any summer pruning until the bushes are a few years old and have started to crop.

Above: *Nick out any buds that you see among the roots of the plant. If left in place, they would produce unwanted suckers later on.*

Pruning a mature redcurrant bush

1 To prune an established bush, remove any low, broken or crossing branches, plus any that are clearly causing overcrowding.

2 Secateurs are normally perfectly adequate for pruning currants, but if you need to remove quite thick branches, then loppers are easier.

1 Start with a strong, one-year-old bush. As it is best grown on a short 'leg', remove any shoots that are less than about 5in(13cm) from the roots.

2 Make the planting hole wide enough to take the spread-out root system and deep enough to leave the planted bush just deeper than before.

3 After planting, remove weak shoots. Cut back strong but badly placed shoots to 1in(2.5cm). Shorten remaining shoots by half their length.

4 Four branches pointing in the right direction form the basic shape. In a year's time there will be eight and this is often enough.

3 There must be a reason for every pruning cut you make and it is normally to do with the shape of the bush or its cropping potential.

4 Shorten the branch leaders (the year-old top section) by half and cut back unwanted side shoots to about 2in(5cm).

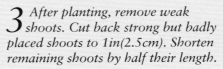

A cluster of fruit buds. Pruning will encourage more buds to form. Do not cut these buds off.

Above: 'Jonkheer van Tets' is a heavy-cropping redcurrant variety. It is very early and produces high-quality fruit. It is widely available for garden use.

Pruning gooseberries

One of the best ways of growing gooseberries is as cordons trained to a wall or fence or grow them in the open up canes. They are much easier to look after than bushes, the dessert varieties ripen better and you are less likely to be scratched. You can grow cordons with just one vertical shoot, or double or multiple cordons with two or more shoots. Single cordons are the quickest to reach the desired height but you need many more plants for a given length of fence. Another unusual shape is the standard, which is just a bush on top of a 3-4ft(90-120cm) stem. Ordinary bushes take up rather a lot of room and are not as easy to maintain. 'Careless' or 'Invicta' are the most prolific cookers, with 'Leveller' an excellent all-round dessert variety. For the biggest and best dessert gooseberries, prune both cordons and bushes in early summer. That is also the time to thin out the fruits to one per cluster, using the thinnings for cooking. Summer pruning simply involves cutting back the new shoots (those you do not want for extension growth) to five leaves, about 5in(13cm) long. Summer pruning improves the berry size and color of dessert varieties and the crop weight of cookers. Early to midsummer is the normal and the most beneficial time to summer prune. Because you are removing the soft growth at the end of the shoots, which is the part most susceptible to attack by mildew, summer pruning also helps to control this disease.

Below: Gooseberries as single or double stem cordons is a terrific way of growing them if space is limited. They also make an excellent subject for creating a useful and attractive barrier between sections of the garden. Midsummer pruning is a standard procedure with cordons.

Pruning a newly planted gooseberry

Before planting a young gooseberry bush such as this, remove any shoots that are closer than about 5in(13cm) to the roots, as well as any buds among the roots. Plant the bush firmly, leaving a clear leg of 5-6in (13-15cm) between the ground and the first branch. Nick out any buds on the leg. To give of their best, gooseberries need good soil conditions. This is especially true of dessert varieties, which are grown to a larger size than cookers.

1 After planting, prune the bush by removing any weak shoots, cutting back misplaced ones and shortening the rest by roughly half their length.

2 Pruning stimulates side shoots, so that the original four or five 'branches' give rise to eight to ten after the first growing season.

Tie these shoots as close to the horizontal as possible.

3 For a U-cordon (with two upright stems) prune back the bush to two strong shoots growing out opposite each other. Bend them down carefully.

1 *A mature, unpruned gooseberry bush in winter needs fairly drastic treatment. Remove all the shoots and branches growing too low or too far out. Crossing branches and those crowding others must also go. The thorns on the bush are very sharp, so wear thick gloves to protect yourself as you work.*

2 *Once the framework is tamed and tidied up, begin shortening all the branch leaders (young shoots on the end of each branch) to half their length.*

Above: Following a heavy set, fruit thinning in early summer, by removing every other fruit, will greatly increase the size of this dessert variety, 'Whitesmith'. The thinnings can be used in the kitchen. Do not thin out cooking varieties; the aim with them is crop weight, not quality.

3 *Shorten side shoots on existing spurs or growing straight from main branches to 3in(7.5cm) to an upward- or outward-pointing bud.*

4 *The bush is well equipped to carry heavy crops without collapsing under the strain. Upright training counteracts the gooseberry's natural weeping habit.*

Raspberries

Raspberries are a popular and easy-to-grow soft fruit. The most convenient way to grow them is in rows in the vegetable garden, although by planting them in groups of three it is quite possible to grow just a few in mixed borders or elsewhere tied to stakes. There are two types of raspberry: summer-fruiting and fall-fruiting. Apart from the obvious difference, the main one is that the fall varieties produce canes that fruit later in the same season, whereas the canes of summer varieties grow during the first year and fruit in the summer of the second year.

Each cane carries just one crop of fruit and the pruning strategy is based on this. With summer varieties, cut down the fruited canes straight after fruiting and tie in the new ones to the wires in their place. All the canes of the fall varieties fruit together. Once they have fruited, leave them until new ones start to appear above ground in the following spring and then cut all the previous year's canes to the ground.

Above: Fall-fruiting raspberries, such as this 'Autumn Bliss', are the answer for lovers of fresh fruit. They extend the raspberry season into early winter.

1 *Plant the canes 15in(38cm) apart, so that all the roots and any buds on them are below the surface. These buds will grow out to produce the following year's canes.*

2 *Immediately after planting, cut back the canes leaving them about 10in(25cm) long. This will allow just a few new shoots to grow from them in the following year.*

Some fruit will develop on the side shoots next year. Only allow a very few to grow on.

3 *It is important to have these new shoots on the canes in the next growing season because they will keep the canes alive while more are being sent up from the buds on the roots.*

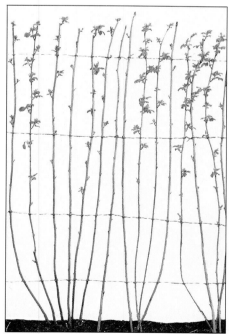

Above: In early spring, the canes from these well-established plants are starting to send out the side shoots that will carry the fruit. Notice the ample spacing and supporting wires.

TRAINING SUMMER-FRUITING RASPBERRIES

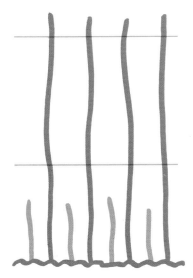

1 During the growing season, the one-year-old canes tied to the wires will be developing fruit. At the same time, new canes are growing that will fruit the following year.

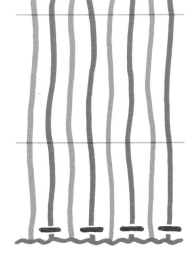

2 By the end of the fruiting season, the new canes will be about as tall as those that fruited. Cut down the fruited canes to leave more room for the new ones to mature and ripen.

3 With the old canes out of the way, tie in the new canes roughly 4in (10cm) apart on the top wire. Choose only the strongest and healthiest ones; cut out any weak or diseased canes.

Left: Raspberries early in the growing season. The fruiting canes are the first to show signs of life. If there has been any winter damage, cut back the tips to the top wire.

Right: If, after tying in, the tops of the new canes reach well above the top wire, bend them over and tie them down to prevent damage. This will also produce some extra fruit.

Below: Fall-fruiting raspberries are spreading and vigorous and should be restricted to a row not more than 18in(45cm) wide from side to side. The only support they need is strong twine down the sides of the row to hold them in.

Blackberries and hybrid cane fruits

Since the introduction of improved thornless varieties, blackberries have become more popular as a garden fruit. There are many ways of training blackberries, but with the exception of 'Loch Ness', all methods involve tying the canes to horizontal wires so that they can be tended and picked easily. One feature common to all systems is that the new canes are kept separate - and usually above - those that are about to fruit to reduce the likelihood of diseases being passed from old to new canes. The less vigorous 'Loch Ness' need not be tied to wires; simply train it onto vertical poles about 8ft(2.4m) tall. It is a good variety for small gardens. With very few exceptions, hybrid cane fruits are all hybrids between blackberries and raspberries. Mostly, they have the long, supple canes of the blackberry but, except for the few thornless variants, their numerous small thorns are more like those of the raspberry. Training systems are similar to those for blackberries. Hybrids are sometimes damaged by a hard winter, so in cold areas tie the new canes together in a bundle before the winter and only release them for tying in properly when the worst weather is past. The bundled canes protect each other. Prune the hybrid berries by cutting out the fruited canes soon after fruiting is over. Hybrid cane fruits include the tasty loganberry, the tayberry, sunberry, marionberry, boysenberry and the recently introduced tummelberry.

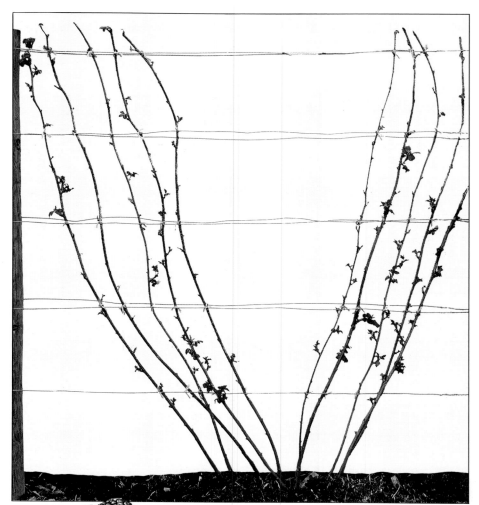

Above: For less vigorous hybrids, such as this loganberry, a fan system of training is ideal. The new canes are trained up the gap in the center between this year's fruiting canes to reduce the risk of spreading disease.

Left: 'Fantasia' is immensely vigorous and thorny, but crops prodigiously and has an excellent flavor. It freezes well, but some berries are apt to go red on freezing. This does not adversely affect the flavor, but the red color remains even after cooking.

Left: *Like the original hybrid, the loganberry, this tayberry is a cross between a raspberry and a blackberry. However, it is far higher yielding and better able to withstand winter cold.*

Left: *Although it is a hybrid cane fruit, the boysenberry, an American variety, has many of the characteristics of the blackberry. Both the color and the flavor resemble it. Crops are heavy, though less so in the thornless form.*

Below: *Cane fruits vary greatly in vigor and the stiffness of their canes. This thornless boysenberry has tall, supple canes, so the two-way rope system is the best way to train it.*

TRAINING BLACKBERRIES AND HYBRID CANE FRUITS

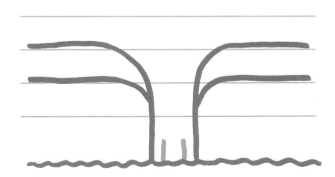

1 Make provision for the new canes to grow up the middle of the plant to lessen the risk of disease infecting them from the older canes.

2 Tie the new canes to the top wire to keep them out of the way. After fruiting is over, cut the cropping canes down.

3 Bring the new canes down from the top wire and tie them in to replace the previous fruiting canes. Picking the fruit will be easier here.

Index

Page numbers in **bold** indicate major text references. Page numbers in *italics* indicate captions and annotations to photographs. Other text entries are shown in normal type.

Credits

The majority of the photographs featured in this book have been taken by Neil Sutherland and are © Colour Library Books. The publishers wish to thank the following photographers for providing additional photographs, credited here by page number and position on the page, i.e. (B)Bottom, (T)Top, (C)Center, (BL)Bottom left, etc.

Gillian Beckett: 53((TR)
Peter Blackburne-Maze: 67(CR), 70(TR), 86(T), 87(BR), 88(B), 89(R)
Pat Brindley: Half-title page, 67(TL), 69(TC), 74(BR), 87(BL)
Eric Crichton: 22(TR), 23(T), 28(BR), 29(TC,BC,BR), 37(BR), 41(TR), 42(BR), 43(TR), 44(BL), 46(TR), 47(TL,TR), 48(TL,R), 49(BL), 72(BR), 75(L), 81(TL), 89(TL), 89(CL)
John Glover: 22(BL,BR), 23(CL,BL,R), 42(L,TR), 53(BR), 55(TR), 57(CL), 62(BL), 63(BL), 66(BL), 67(TR), 68(BL,TR)
S & O Mathews: 10, 22(CL), 37(BL), 40(BL,BR), 44(R), 52(BR), 56(TR), 58(BL,BR), 58-9(T), 59(BL), 60(BR), 61(TR), 62(TR,BC), 63(BC), 64-65(BC), 69TR)
Clive Nichols: Copyright page (Mottifont Abbey, Hampshire), 33(TR,Osler Road, Oxford), 36(BR, Bourton House, Glos.), 38(BR, The Old Rectory, Northants.), 49(TL), 57(TR, Copton Ash, Kent), 66(C), 67(BL, Bramden House Garden, Hampshire), 74(BL, The Old Rectory, Northants.)
Photos Horticulatural Picture Library: 40(TR), 44(TL), 63(TL), 69(BL), 84(T)
Harry Smith Horticultural Photographic Collection: 29(TL)

Acknowledgments

The publishers would like to thank the following people and organizations for their help during the preparation of this book:
Brinsbury College - The West Sussex College of Agriculture and Horticulture; Burton McCall Ltd. for Felco saws and secateurs; Court Lane Nursery, Hadlow College, Kent; Darlac Products for Ratchet 2000 heavy duty secateurs; The Royal Horticultural Society Garden at Wisley, Surrey; Murrell's Nursery, West Sussex.